SILVER LININGS

Blessings

Gifts From God

new seasons™

Cover illustration: Linda Montgomery

Illustrators: Vivian Browning, Marian Hirsch, Steven Mach, Linda Montgomery

Acknowledgments:
Pages 14–16, 182: Excerpts from *See You at the House* by Robert Benson, copyright © 1986, Word Publishing, Nashville, Tennessee. All rights reserved.

Pages 18–19, 111: Excerpts from *Give Happiness a Chance* by Phil Bosmans, copyright © 1980. Used with permission from the author.

Pages 38–41: "Reward of Mercy" by A. J. Cronin. Reprinted with permission from the September 1941 *Reader's Digest*. Copyright © 1941 by The Reader's Digest Association, Inc.

Page 42: Excerpt from *Till Armageddon: A Perspective on Suffering* by Billy Graham, copyright © 1981, Word Publishing, Nashville, Tennessee. All rights reserved.

Page 49: Excerpt from *She Wanted to Read* by Ella Kaiser Carruth, copyright © 1966 by Abingdon Press. Used by permission.

Page 133: Excerpt from *Answers to Life's Problems* by Billy Graham, copyright © 1981, Word Publishing, Nashville, Tennessee. All rights reserved.

Scripture quotations are from the *New Revised Standard Version* of the Bible, copyright © 1989, by the Division of Christian Education of the National Council of the Churches of Christ in the United States of America, and are used by permission. All rights reserved. Marked translations are *New International Version* (NIV), *New Living Translation* (NLT), *The Living Bible* (TLB), and *King James Version* (KJV).

New Seasons is a trademark of Publications International, Ltd.

Contents

A Bounty of Blessings

*W*hen we stop to consider all that we have, we will discover that God has blessed us with many wonderful and precious gifts. As our Creator, he has placed us in a fascinating world, where we can enjoy the birds soaring in the skies, the flowers blooming in the meadows, the streams running down the mountains, and the breeze cooling us during a sunny day. As our heavenly Father, he has given us family and friends, who have encouraged us to follow our dreams, rejoiced with us in our triumphs, and stood beside us during hard times. And as our Lord, he has endowed us with those inner traits that only he can give, such as his joy and his peace and his love.

Blessings: Gifts From God describes many of these cherished gifts from God, and the writers of this book have contributed their insights on how God has personally blessed them, doing so in a variety of ways. Whether through a story, a poem, a song, a prayer, or a thoughtful obser-vation, they will inspire you to realize that you are truly blessed by God. In addition, the selected verses from Scripture will help you know that God wants you to receive these blessings he has waiting for you.

The writer of Proverbs stated, "The blessing of the Lord makes rich" (Proverbs 10:22). Indeed, the wealthiest people are those who enjoy the blessings of God, and those who know not those blessings are poor, even if they possess the riches of the world. Moreover, we need not earn those blessings as one would purchase a mansion or a yacht. We need only ask God and be faithful to his teachings, and he will pour the blessings we need upon us. So read this book and claim the blessings others have known in their walk with God.

*"Instead of a gem or a flower,
cast the gift of a lovely thought
into the heart of a friend."*

—GEORGE MACDONALD

Grateful for
Loved Ones

Blessed Be the Tie That Binds

*Friends and family members are often
separated by distance. But we know that
God is the tie that binds us all together,
no matter where we are.*

Celebrate Love

*May you enjoy all the streams of love that flow
into your life: The love from family and friends;
the love from parents and children; the love
from pets; and the love from God. Celebrate
love all day long. For it is the breath of your
existence and the best of all reasons for living.*

*A friend loves at all times,
and kinsfolk are born
to share adversity.*

—PROVERBS 17:17

*D*ear brothers and sisters, what's the use of saying you have faith if you don't prove it by your actions? That kind of faith can't save anyone. Suppose you see a brother or sister who needs food or clothing, and you say, "Well, good-bye and God bless you; stay warm and eat well"—but then you don't give that person any food or clothing. What good does that do? So you see, it isn't enough just to have faith. Faith that doesn't show itself by good deeds is no faith at all— it is dead and useless.

—JAMES 2:15–17 (NLT)

Not Alone

*Go in peace. You are not alone in the world.
Rejoice in friendships, fellowships,
acquaintances, parties, and get-togethers of
every kind. You are not alone. Rejoice.*

Neighborly Blessing

*Bless my neighbor today. But keep me from
telling him that I've got his good in mind. Only
let him discover it in my smile, in my
encouraging words, and in my helping hand.*

*D*on't get tired of doing what is good. Don't get discouraged and give up, for we will reap a harvest of blessing at the appropriate time. Whenever we have the opportunity, we should do good to everyone, especially to our Christian brothers and sisters.

—GALATIANS 6:9–10 (NLT)

Be Blessed

May you find joy and satisfaction in your family life: In building a home and setting up a residence—be blessed! In finding a job and working diligently—be blessed! In taking care of little ones and making friends in the neighborhood—be blessed! In seeking God for all your help and guidance, bringing every care to him. Yes, I pray, may you indeed be blessed.

The Power of Affirmation

*G*od has given each person a storehouse of wisdom and creativity. But to fully tap into our potential, we have to believe in ourselves—and it helps to know that others believe in us, too. In fact, it can make all the difference.

We all know how very much it means to be believed in. There was a study done by a group of researchers from Harvard. They would go to elementary school teachers at the beginning of the school year and tell them that they had designed a test which could prove most helpful to them. The results would correctly predict which students were going to grow intellectually during the coming school year. Someone called it "The Harvard Test of Intellectual Spurts" because it told which students were going to "spurt" that year. The researchers promised it would pick out the right students and it was very, very accurate.

Given permission, they administered, unbeknownst to the teacher, an old, obsolete I.Q. test. When the students had finished the test, the papers were collected and the researchers threw them in the wastebasket. Then they picked five names at random from the roll book and sat down with the teachers and said, "Now these are the students in your class who are going to have a very good year. Watch these kids. One of them is Rachel Smith," they informed the teacher.

"Rachel Smith?" the teacher replied incredulously, "She wouldn't 'spurt' if you shot her from a cannon. I have had two of her brothers and each one of the Smiths is dumber than the last." But the educators maintained that the test hardly ever was wrong in its findings and that Rachel's progress in the ensuing year could be readily observed.

You can imagine what happened that semester, can't you? Yes, you can. Rachel never had a chance to be her same old self. Under a barrage of "Rachel, would you write this on the board this morning," "Rachel will lead the line to the lunch room today," "Is that a new dress, Rachel? It sure is pretty," "Thank you, Rachel, that was very good," Rachel 'spurted' all over the place. And so did every name they put on that list.

According to the Apostle Paul, every one of our names belongs on a list like that. We are all "God's chosen people, holy and dearly loved." I think one of my all-time favorite quotes is from a little boy in elementary school who said,

"My teacher thought I was smarter than I wuz. So I wuz!" And all of us need to be in a group that believes we are smarter and better and more gifted than we have ever dared to think we were. For this is one of the ways that each of us will begin to hear the calling voice of God.

We need to see that we are to be giving life even as we are receiving it, that we are to be nurturing even as we are being nurtured, that we are to be healing even as we are being healed.

One of the things that the hand on our shoulder is saying to each of us is a deep, affirmative, "I believe in you." And we should be saying to the one whose shoulder we are touching, "I believe in who you are, and what you can become, because of the gifts that God has put within you."

—BOB BENSON, *SEE YOU AT THE HOUSE*

Together

Bless this partnership, God,
the friendship of her and me.
And remind us both: Every gathering
of two is really a fellowship of three.

Tapestry of Marriage

*From our first shy "I love you" to today's
public vow, you pulled us like two strands from
the tangled world and brought us together.
Each is distinct and colorful but joined now so
lovingly that the sorrow—and joy likewise—
of one will be felt by the other.*

Love and Friendship

A healthy friendship enhances our lives. What a blessing to have someone who wants to share all our joys and sorrows. We should continually strive to be the kind of friend God would like us to be—and the kind of friend that we would like to have.

Love from friendship—
this love leads to light,
to peace and to deep joy.
This love never harms people.
It does not possess for itself.
It leaves the other person free.
And when it finds expression
in physical tenderness,
it stays pure.
But when one person wants
to possess another for himself
   alone,
for his own satisfaction,
he destroys the person he thinks
   he loves.

And destroys the friendship.
True, you will never be capable
of a totally unselfish friendship.
But you must always keep trying.

—PHIL BOSMANS, "LOVE AND FRIENDSHIP,"
GIVE HAPPINESS A CHANCE

Don't Be a Stranger!

May you leave home
with a good feeling in your heart.
Fond memories,
a willingness to write,
a desire to return for friendly
    visits.
You are loved here.
Don't be a stranger!
May you cut the apron strings,
though, as you need to.
Growth is our wish for you.
And this is God's plan for
    you, too.
Receive his blessing!

Blessed Teens

*T*his birthday, Lord, my child becomes a teen. Surely it's just the smoke of 13 candles making me cry. But, O Lord, wasn't it just yesterday that there was just a single candle?

From before that day to this, I've trusted you. I ask you now to bless the youthful drive to risk making choices; the struggle to be heard; the changing body, moods, and mind. Bless—and this is hardest for me to say—the urge for independence.

Bless me with ears to listen, a shoulder to lean on, and the good sense to build bridges, not walls.

Setting Out

*A*s you leave home now, may you know that your whole family will be keeping you in their thoughts and prayers. Let this sustain you in the tough times; let it keep you anchored in the joyful times, too. Seeing you launch out on your own is so good! Enjoy the blessing of independence, and come home whenever you can. The welcome mat is out, the porch light on. And our same God will take care of you, just as he has watched over us all, for all these years.

For Those Who Can't Speak

Bless the pet in this house. I don't know whether or not they have souls, but I do know they have needs and emotions, times of playfulness and times of fear. Keep them in safety throughout this night. And give me a compassionate heart and a caring attitude toward them always.

Blessing New Parents

*May you find that starting a family was
your best decision ever. Look into the eyes of
this little one and be blessed. You're due to
receive a lot of love. Only be sure you
give even more in return.*

Message of Giggles

Bless the children, God of little ones,
with their giggles and wide-eyed awe, their
awakening assumption that today will be chock-
full of surprises, learning, and love. Neither
missing nor wasting a minute, they take
nothing for granted, a message that blesses us.
We will go and do likewise.

Blessing for a Newborn

Bless this little one of so
  few days.
May he be prosperous in
  all his ways.
Healthy in body and mind,
Growing strong and kind.
Bless this little one through
  all his days.

The Apple of My Eye

Guard me as the apple of the eye;
hide me in the shadow of your wings.
—Psalm 17:8

When my daughter Margaret was born, I was as proud as any dad could be. It was June, and I was teaching elementary school at the time. That fall I would hold her up and proudly show her off to the parents of my new students.

Margaret was "the apple of my eye" in the way that we usually use the term. I wanted to look at her all the time. I wanted everyone to know she was mine. Now, 20 years later, I still like to look at her. I'll watch her from across a room, talking with strangers or playing with children or reading a book. She has grown into a lovely young woman, and I think I may be just as proud of Margaret now as I was then, although not nearly as possessive.

That's because the way I see Margaret has changed, as has my understanding of the phrase "apple of my eye." I used to think it merely meant pride, like a farmer showing off a good crop or a dad's holding out his child for all the world to see. But the Hebrew term trans-

lated five times in the King James Version of
the Bible as "apple of the eye" has nothing to
do with fruit.

It actually means "little man," referring to
the image we see if we look closely into the eyes
of someone else. Another meaning is "daughter," in perhaps the same sense. The Hebrews
meant it as the pupil of the eye, a place where
we can see a reflection of ourselves and through
which we see the things we love. Of course,
that's what I see when I see Margaret now, a
kinder and—thankfully—prettier version of
myself. I still brag about her a little and embarrass her a lot. That's because who she is reflects
well on me and on the contributions I've made
in her life.

It's comforting to think of God seeing us
that way—as the apple of his eye, a reflection of
himself. We bear his image; we are his sons and
daughters. So he looks on us with pride and
holds us up for the angels to see. "Look, this is
my child, the apple of my eye."

He shielded him, cared for him,
guarded him as the apple
of his eye.

—Deuteronomy 32:10

Blessings on the
Anniversary Couple

There is no greater mystery than love, Lord of covenants and promises. We are in its presence on this anniversary day. Bless those who live, day after day after ordinary day, within the fullness of married love, surely one of the greatest mysteries. Bless them as they honor their past, even while they create a future. Let them bask in the pleasures and applause of today, when we bow before their accomplishments which, like the rings we read inside trees, are an inspiration and blessing to us all.

Blessings for Grandparents on Their Day

They've created a new holiday, Lord, a day to honor the grandparents who tended us so well. Pause with us as we play again in the dusty lanes of childhood at Grandma and Grandpa's house. Bless these bigger-than-life companions who helped us bridge home and away, childhood and maturity. In their footsteps, we made the journey. Thank you for such a heritage and a day on which to express our gratitude.

How very good and pleasant it
is when kindred live together
in unity!

—PSALM 133:1

Yours, Mine, and Ours:
Blessing for a Step-Family

*We come as pieces of a puzzle that can't quite
fit together. Bless and lead us, a family in the
making, God of unity. Turn us around, sort us
out, and reassemble us in a satisfying whole.*

Suddenly a Family

*May you fall in love with this new family
more and more each day. No, you weren't
planning to suddenly have children, but here
they are—a gift from your new spouse.
A step-parent isn't accepted right from the start,
so be patient. Love will grow between you as
you look out for one another's inner needs.
Blessings upon you and the children.
God grant that you be all a family can be.*

Blessing a Step-Family

*B*less this gathering of what, at first glance,
looks like a mismatched party, encircling
God, for we want to become a family. Guide us
as we *step* closer to one another, but not so
close as to crowd. Heal wounds from the past
events that made this union possible.

Bless the children with the courage to try
new relatives, new traditions, new homes.
Empower them in their anger, helping them
know that it is OK and that tears are healing.
Assure them that they have the strength to live
in two worlds and hearts big enough to love
others. Make us, the step-adults, worthy of this
love, for it comes at great cost. Help us respect
previous traditions and loves and not *step* too
close in our need to belong. For even in the
midst of celebrating, there is mourning.

Remind us to take *baby steps* as we become
all you have in mind. Your presence will be our
companion, your love our protection, and your
wisdom our guidance in this awesome respon-
sibility. *Step* closer, loving God, and lead us.

Sacrificial Love

O. Henry's timeless story is about much more than beautiful hair combs and a platinum fob watch chain. It's about true love's willingness to give everything—even those things that are most treasured—for those we love.

"Jim, darling," she cried, "don't look at me that way. I had my hair cut off and sold it because I couldn't have lived through Christmas without giving you a present. It'll grow out again—you won't mind, will you? I just had to do it. My hair grows awfully fast. Say 'Merry Christmas!' Jim, and let's be happy. You don't know what a nice—what a beautiful nice gift I've got for you."

"You've cut off your hair?" asked Jim, laboriously, as if he had not arrived at that patent fact yet even after the hardest mental labor.

"Cut it off and sold it," said Della. "Don't you like me just as well, anyhow? I'm me without my hair, ain't I?"

Jim looked about the room curiously.

"You say your hair is gone?" he said, with an air almost of idiocy.

"You needn't look for it," said Della. "It's sold, I tell you—sold and gone, too. It's Christmas even, boy. Be good to me, for it went for you. Maybe the hairs of my head were numbered," she went on with a sudden serious sweetness, "but nobody could count my love for you. Shall I put the chops on, Jim?"

Out of his trance, Jim seemed quickly to wake. He enfolded Della . . .

Jim drew a package from his overcoat pocket and threw it upon the table.

"Don't make any mistake, Dell," he said, "about me. I don't think there's anything in the way of a haircut or a shave or a shampoo that could make me like my girl any less. But if you'll unwrap that package you may see why you had me going a while at first."

White fingers and nimble tore at the string and paper. And then an ecstatic scream of joy; and then, alas! a quick feminine change to hysterical tears and wails, necessitating the immediate employment of all the comforting powers of the lord of the flat.

For there lay The Combs—the set of combs, side and back, that Della worshipped for long in a Broadway window. Beautiful combs, pure tortoise shell, with jeweled rims—just the shade to wear in the beautiful vanished hair. They were expensive combs, she knew, and her heart had simply craved and yearned over them without the least hope of possession. And now, they were hers, but the tresses that should have adorned the coveted adornments were gone.

But she hugged them to her bosom, and at length she was able to look with dim eyes and a smile and say: "My hair grows so fast, Jim!"

And then Della leaped up like a little singed cat and cried, "Oh, oh!"

Jim had not yet seen his beautiful present. She held it out to him eagerly upon her open palm. The dull precious metal seemed to flash with a reflection of her bright and ardent spirit.

"Isn't it a dandy, Jim? I hunted all over town to find it. You'll have to look at the time a hundred times a day now. Give me your watch. I want to see how it looks on it."

Instead of obeying, Jim tumbled down on the couch and put his hands under the back of his head and smiled.

"Dell," said he, "let's put our Christmas presents away and keep 'em a while. They're too nice to use just at present. I sold the watch to get the money to buy your combs. And now suppose you put the chops on."

The magi, as you know, were wise men—wonderfully wise men—who brought gifts to the Babe in the manger. They invented the art of giving Christmas presents. Being wise, their gifts were no doubt wise ones, possibly bearing the privilege of exchange in case of duplication. And here I have lamely related to you the uneventful chronicle of two foolish children in a flat who most unwisely sacrificed for each other the greatest treasures of their house. But in a last word to the wise of these days let it be said that of all who give gifts these two were the wisest. Of all who give and receive gifts, such as they are wisest. Everywhere they are wisest. They are the magi.

—O. HENRY, "THE GIFT OF THE MAGI"

Cheering Section

*Bless those who mentor, model, and
cheer me on, Lord, urging me toward goals
I set, applauding as I reach them, and
nourishing me to try again when I don't.
Remind me to be a cheerleader. I plan to say
thanks to those who are mine.*

True Love

**True love is not based on outer appearances. It
goes deeper and is a matter of the heart. Sometimes love is tested to see if it is real. It's inspir-
ing when someone passes the test!**

*O*ne day when I was in Brooklyn, I saw a
young man going along the street without any arms. A friend who was with me
pointed him out and told me his story. When
the war broke out, he felt it to be his duty to
enlist and go to the front. He was engaged to
be married, and while in the army letters passed
frequently between him and his intended wife.

After the battle of the Wilderness, the young lady looked anxiously for the accustomed letter. For a little while no letter was received. At last one came in a strange hand. She opened it with trembling fingers and read these words: "We have fought a terrible battle. I have been wounded so awfully that I shall never be able to support you. A friend writes this for me. I love you more tenderly than ever, but I release you from your promise. I will not ask you to join your life with the maimed life of mine."

That letter was never answered. The next train that left, the young lady was on it. She went to the hospital. She found out the number of his cot, and she went down the aisle between the long rows of the wounded men. At last she saw the number, and, hurrying to his side, she threw her arms around his neck and said: "I'll not desert you. I'll take care of you." He did not resist her love. They were married, and there is no happier couple than this one.

—DWIGHT L. MOODY,
ANECDOTES AND ILLUSTRATIONS OF DWIGHT L. MOODY

*You are an Alpha and Omega
God, the parentheses between
which we live, move, and
have our being. Bless our
comings and goings.*

The Life We Have

Reward of Mercy

While we are all familiar with systems of punishment and reward, a wise person will know when to dispense justice and when to be merciful.

I was raised in the strict tradition that if one did wrong, one should be punished for it. That was called justice.

In 1921, as a young doctor, I took over the post of medical officer to a fever hospital in a bleak and isolated district of Northumberland. One winter evening, shortly after my arrival, a diphtheria case was admitted: a little boy of six so desperately choked with membrane that an immediate tracheotomy offered the only slender chance of saving him.

Painfully inexperienced, I had never attempted this simple but crucial operation. As I stood in the bare, lamp-lit ward and watched the old sister and the only nurse—a junior probationer—place the gasping child upon the table, I felt myself trembling, cold and sick.

I began the operation: a nervous incision into that thin, congested throat. As I fumbled on, conscious of my own incompetence, a resolution to succeed, to save this suffocating child took possession of me. At last the stem of the trachea showed white and shining under my sweat-dimmed eyes. I slit it and a rush of air filled the child's struggling chest. Again and again the tortured lungs expanded. As new strength flooded the exhausted little body, I could have cried aloud in relief. Quickly I slipped in the tracheotomy tube, completed the sutures, and saw the child comfortable in his steam-tented bed. I went back to my own quarters in a glow of triumphant joy.

Four hours later, at two o'clock in the morning, I was roused by a frantic knocking at my door. It was the young nurse. White-faced, hysterical, she stammered: "Doctor, doctor, come quickly."

She had drowsed off by the child's cot and awakened to find that the tube had become blocked. Instead of following instructions and clearing the tube of membrane, a matter of nursing routine, she had lost her head and committed the unpardonable sin of bolting in panic. When I got to the ward, the child was dead. Nothing we could do was of any avail.

The sense of loss, the needless, culpable waste of human life overwhelmed me. Worst of all was the thought of my precious case wrecked by the blundering negligence of a frightened nurse. My anger blazed at white heat. Of course, her career was finished. I would send a report to the County Health Board, and she would be kicked out of the hospital, expelled from the nursing body to which she belonged.

That evening I dipped my pen in vitriol and wrote the indictment. I summoned her and read it to her in a voice burning with indignation.

She heard me in pitiful silence. She was a raw Welsh girl of about 19, thin and rather gawky, with a nervous tremor of her cheek. Anemic and undernourished, she was now half-fainting with shame and misery.

Her failure to make any sort of excuse—she might with some justification have pleaded that she was worn out with overwork—stung me into exclaiming: "Have you nothing to say?"

She shook her head wanly. Suddenly she stammered: "Give me another chance."

I was taken aback. The idea had never entered my head. My sole thought was to make her pay for what she had done. I stared at her, then dismissed her curtly. I signed and sealed my report.

All through that night I was strangely troubled. "Give me another chance." A queer echo kept drumming in my head, an echo which whispered that my justice, that all justice was no more than a primitive desire for revenge. Angrily I told myself not to be a fool.

Yet next morning I went to the letter rack and tore up my report.

That was 20 years ago. Today the nurse who erred so fatally is matron of the largest children's home in Wales. Her career has been a model of service and devotion. Only a week ago I received a photograph showing a middle-aged woman in matron's uniform, surrounded by children, in an air-raid shelter. She looks harassed and weary; but the childish eyes which gaze at her are filled with trust and love.

"Forgive us our trespasses as we forgive those that trespass against us." It's hard to practice that simple prayer. But, even in this life, it pays.

—A. J. CRONIN, IN *READER'S DIGEST,*
SEPTEMBER 1941

*C*omfort and prosperity have
never enriched the world as
adversity has done. Out of pain
and problems have come the
sweetest songs, the most
poignant poems, the most
gripping stories. Out of suffering
and tears have come the greatest
spirits and most blessed lives.

—BILLY GRAHAM, *TILL ARMAGEDDON*

Blessings for a New Employee

*M*ay *you enjoy your new job. Slide into it
with a calm heart. Find the pencil sharpener.
Don't become overwhelmed with all your new
responsibilities. God can help you approach
each task, one at a time, starting on your
very first day. Look to him and your new
friends for all you need. Blessings!*

A New Beginning

What a blessing to have a second
chance!
Grant me the wisdom to use this
opportunity wisely.
And save me from the fear that
I'll fall into the same old traps
as last time.
This is a brand-new day, a whole
new beginning. Fantastic!

Blessed is he who has found
his work; let him ask no other
blessedness. He has a work,
a life-purpose; he has found it
and will follow it.

—THOMAS CARLYLE, *PAST AND PRESENT*

The Blessing of Work

What a blessing, Almighty One, to be able to earn a living for my family! To be free of worry about what they will eat, or what they will wear, or where they will sleep. You have given me so much: house, flowers, table and chairs, even our memories to help us remember these days that are flying by so quickly. Yes, you have blessed me with so much, especially my work.

A Job Well Done

How good to get this promotion! And how I've waited for this day! Now that it is here, I thank you for the chance to savor it. A job well done is a good thing, I know. I will celebrate before your smiling eyes and give you credit, too. Because, after all, everything I am and have comes from your gracious hand.

Leaving a Mark: A Blessing for Jobs

Bless our work, Lord. We long to leave a mark as visible as a building or bridge. We yearn to be connected with what we do and to do something that matters. Show us that what we do is as indelible as a handprint on fresh concrete even though our mark may be in spots no one can see right now except us. Harvest comes in its own sweet time. Bless the marks we leave behind, for with you as our foundation, our work is as essential to the overall structure of life as a concrete pillar.

On the Blessings of Life

Go forth in the joy of the Lord,
    knowing how blessed you are.
Celebrate the beauty of nature
    around you.
Celebrate the goodness of
    fellowship with others.
Celebrate the opportunity to
    grow and learn and take up
    the challenge of each new day.
Most of all: Celebrate your life.
How blessed you are!

*A*nd let us not get tired of doing
what is right, for after a while we
will reap a harvest of blessing if we
don't get discouraged and give up.

—Galatians 6:9 (TLB)

Answering the Call

*W*ork is good right now, God of all labor, and I think I know why: You and I are working together. Is this what it is to be *called*? I think it must be, for you are the source of my talents, for which I am grateful. Through the support of others—gifted teachers, mentors, and leaders, and through those willing to take a chance on me despite the odds, you have always been present, and I am grateful for that, too.

Although this sense that I am doing what you intend for me is usually just a thrilling, split-second awareness, O God, it is enough to keep me going when I am tired, frustrated, and unclear about my next step. Our companionship of call to vocation is not an instant process, but rather a shared journey. Keep me listening and watching.

I am glad we share this working venture, for on the job and off, I am blessed.

Bless This Mess

*T*he house is a mess, Lord, and because of it, my attitude is a matching mood. Like hand-writing on the wall of my grumpy heart, I got your message: It's far wiser to hunt for first crocuses on spring days than lost socks in the laundry and to chase giggles rising from a child's soul like dandelion fluff than dust balls beneath beds. Bless, O Lord, this wonder-ful mess, and send me out to play.

The Blessing of Letting Go

*H*ow blessed the one who can walk this journey
*with a light grip on everything! For all will be
released, sooner or later. And I wish to practice
now, Lord—moment by moment—the letting go.*

Faith Brings Rewards

*I*n 1949 the trustees of Rollins College in Winter Park, Florida, asked Mary Bethune to accept an honorary degree.

Mary received the first honorary degree ever given to a Negro by a white southern college.

She stood as tall as she could as she listened to President Holt say, "Mary McLeod Bethune, I deem it one of the highest privileges that has come to me as President of Rollins College to do honor to you this morning. I am proud that Rollins is, I am told, the first white college in the South to bestow an honorary degree on one of your race. You have in your own person demonstrated that from the humblest beginnings and through the most adverse circumstances it is still possible for one who has the will, the intelligence, the courage, and the never-failing faith in God and in your fellow man to rise from the humblest cabin in the land to a place of honor and influence among the world's eminent...."

—Ella Kaiser Carruth, *She Wanted to Read: The Story of Mary McLeod Bethune*

Not-So-Empty Nest

*An empty nest. Finally! Now it's time
for dinner and dancing, long walks in
the park, visits with old friends, full
concentration on fulfilling work, a round of
golf, and a little fishing, too. I never thought it
would be so calm and quiet around here.
What a blessing! Thank you, God.*

Blessing for Old Age

*Bless my milestones from first grandchild
to last day in my own home and, dear Lord,
the ordinary days between. Bless my tears,
for they nourish new fields where I find joy in
the harvest. Bless my aging, a rebirth into
whom you yet call me to be.*

For One Who Lives Well

Blessed are you who know how to
celebrate the goodness of life.
Blessed because you choose to see the
grace above and beyond the pain.
Blessed because you see a potential
friend in every stranger you meet.
Blessed because you know the
darkest clouds have brilliant silver
linings.
And most blessed because: All you
ever knew of the half-empty glass
was that it was almost full.

A Beautiful Gift

*How marvelous our bodies! May we
care for them today with all the reverence and
honor we might extend toward any
cherished gift from God.*

A Single Blessing

My God, I thank you for the blessings of the single life.

One of your plans was for people to get married and have children. But I know that your good and perfect will is also for some of us to be single and not have children.

For this life I thank you. For the gift to be free to learn to love without clinging, to seek relationships without owning, and to offer my love and kindness among many friends.

Yes, Lord, at times I am lonely, like all people can be. So I ask you to fill those times of emptiness with your presence. Enter into the barren places with your refreshing water of life.

And as I continue on this path—living by myself—keep my friends and family close, no matter how far away they live. Give me peace in my daily work, joy in the pursuit of wholeness, and comfort in the solitary nights. And please continue to grant me a giving heart. For I know, Lord, I am blessed.

Bless the Ruts in the Yard

I am grateful, O God, that your standards run more to how we're loving you and one another than how we appear. If you judged on lawns, I would be out in the cold!

Mine is the yard where kids gather. Ball games, sprinkler tag's muddy marathons, snow fort and tree house constructions, car tinkerings and bike repair—they all happen here.

Bless my rutted, littered lawn, wise Creator. It's the most beautiful landscape, dotted as it is with children who will be grown and gone faster than we can say "replant."

Of all good gifts that the Lord
    lets fall,
Is not silence the best of all?
The deep, sweet hush when the
    song is closed,
And every sound but a voiceless
    ghost;
And every sigh, as we listening
    leant,
A breathless quiet of vast
    content?
The laughs we laughed have a
    purer ring
With but their memory echoing;
So of all good gifts that the Lord
    lets fall,
Is not silence the best of all?

—JAMES WHITCOMB RILEY,
    "BEST OF ALL"

Blessed Solitude

*May you recognize today that being
alone is not always being lonely nor that
solitude must always have problem to solve.
With everyone far away, rejoice in
the blessing of your quietness.*

The fear of the Lord is the
beginning of wisdom, and the
knowledge of the Holy One is
insight. For by me your days will
be multiplied, and years will be
added to your life.

—PROVERBS 9:10–11

Life's Many Blessings

*O*ur Lord has showered our lives with many blessings, which we often take for granted. May we take the time to enjoy each blessing and give thanks to him who has blessed us.

Tools

*Bless these tools of my work, Lord.
Keep them sharp and strong and ready to do
my will. And bless these hands, too, that they
might be ready to do all you desire. Thank you
for these blessings you've given me.*

For This Moment

*Bless these next few, short moments in my day,
before the next problem arises. And may I
remember, in all my busy-ness, that the best
time to seek you is always the same:
now, right now.*

Slow Down

*May you find today that, rather than thriving
on the hectic pace of your schedule, just slowing
down a bit can be the greatest of blessings.*

A Lesson in Suffering

May I be blessed in this suffering. May I know
that you can use this thing to show me a
mistaken attitude or a destructive behavior.
In that way, may I be blessed in this suffering,
O Lord, my God.

Near-Miss Blessings

It's the close calls to body, mind, and soul that
do me in, Lord, like crossing railroad tracks
only to see a freight train framed in my
rearview mirror. I'm keeping these moments in
the margins of my heart to remind me to live
each day as a newfound treasure.

Prove Your Faith

True faith in God is demonstrated
when we look for ways to be kind and generous
to those in need.

Blessed is the man
who does not walk in the
   counsel of the wicked
or stand in the way of sinners
or sit in the seat of mockers.
But his delight is in the law of
   the Lord,
and on his law he meditates day
   and night.
He is like a tree planted by
   streams of water,
which yields its fruit in season
and whose leaf does not wither.
Whatever he does prospers.

—Psalm 1 (NIV)

The Blessing in Your Eyes

*When you look around you today,
know the blessing of seeing God in every smiling
face. Reflect that blessing in your own eyes,
silently, with a kind heart.*

The Blessings of Growth Rings

O Lord, bless our life stages, for they read like growth rings on a mighty tree: our beginnings and firsts with their excitement, newness, and anxiety; our middles, full of diligence and commitment and, yes, we confess, sometimes boredom, but also risk and derring-do; our "nexts," the harvests and reapings; the slowing down and freedom.

Present Blessings

*M*ay your thoughts focus much more upon what you *have* than what you *lack* in this trying time. May your heart lay hold of present realities rather than future possibilities. For this moment—the now—is all we are given. Whether we are sick or healthy, this juncture in time is the place we share. Let us be blessed in this moment, needing nothing to change. Let us simply *be* in God's presence, just for this moment.

*F*inally, all of you should be of one mind, full of sympathy toward each other, loving one another with tender hearts and humble minds. Don't repay evil for evil. Don't retaliate when people say unkind things about you. Instead, pay them back with a blessing. That is what God wants you to do, and he will bless you for it.

—1 Peter 3:8–9 (NLT)

Understanding Humility

*L*ike a multi-faceted stone, the humble person's colors shine forth. By their nature, they are able to bear an injustice without retaliating, do one's duty even when one is not watched, keep at the job until it is finished, and make use of criticism without being defeated by it.

At one time true humility was thought to mean thinking negatively of oneself or belittling oneself. But this is neither a correct interpretation, nor is it a current definition. It is more accurate to look at humility as not thinking more highly of oneself than we ought to think: "Be honest in your estimate of yourselves, measuring your value by how much faith God has given you" (Romans 12:3, NLT).

Humility actually means not thinking of oneself, but putting others first. We disregard our rights and ambitions so we can serve God by serving others. Arriving at a place of humility is a result of understanding the biblical advice to "serve each other with humble spirits, for God gives special blessings to those who are humble, but sets himself against those who are proud. If you humble yourselves under the mighty hand of God, in his good time he will lift you up" (1 Peter 5:5-6, TLB).

The major obstacle to humility is pride. Pride and self-will become hindrances to our life of faith when we believe that either God does not care about or does not understand our situations in life. Or we believe that we don't need God's help to live our Christian lives—we think we can look out for ourselves. When pride lures us into living independently of God, the result can be disastrous. The Book of Proverbs is full of warnings about the danger of allowing pride to creep into our lives: "Pride leads to arguments; be humble, take advice and become wise" (Proverbs 13:10, TLB). "Pride ends in destruction; humility ends in honor" (Proverbs 18:12, TLB).

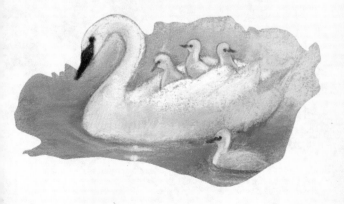

*Lord, thank you for being a
God of new beginnings.
Give me a fresh start today as
I trust in you.*

In His Care

A Good Confession

The chains that have bound me
　　are flung to the wind,
by the mercy of God the poor
　　slave is set free.
And the strong arm of heaven
　　breathes fresh o'er the mind,
like the bright winds of summer
　　that brighten the sea.
I cried out in mercy, and fell on
　　my knees,
and confessed, while my heart
　　with keen sorrow was wrung;
'twas the labor of minutes, and
　　years of disease
fell as fast from my soul as the
　　words from my tongue.
And now, blest be God and the
　　sweet Lord who died!
No deer on the mountain, no
　　bird in the sky,

no dark wave that leaps on the
    dark bounding tide,
is a creature so free or so happy
    as I.

—FREDERICK WILLIAM FARBER

*H*umble yourselves therefore
under the mighty hand of God,
so that he may exalt you in due
time. Cast all your anxiety on
him, because he cares for you.

—1 PETER 5:6–7

Weather Forecast

*We are blessed by your enveloping spirit as
near to us as daily changing weather.
Your comfort touches us like gentle rain and
hushed snow. And, like the sound of thunder
and the glimpse of searing lightning, you
startle us with new opportunities.*

Lay Your Burdens Down

Come to me, all you that are weary and are
carrying heavy burdens, and I will give you rest.
Take my yoke upon you, and learn from me; for
I am gentle and humble in heart, and you will
find rest for your souls. For my yoke is easy,
and my burden is light.
—MATTHEW 11:28–30

*J*esus knew what a yoke was. He and his earthly father, Joseph, probably made them in their carpenter's shop. Basically, a yoke is a wooden frame placed over the neck of two oxen and attached to a plow, sled, or cart. It was different than a harness used on a horse; the yoke was designed to pull against the broad, strong shoulders of a draft animal.

Yet Jesus knew what a yoke was in a figurative sense as well. For centuries, yokes had been used on captives and slaves, and the prophets had compared the oppression Israel experienced to a "yoke of bondage." Hardship and forced labor, servitude and submission: These hardships were not unknown to this tiny nation at the crossroads of the ancient world.

Jesus and his followers had experienced all this at the hands of the Romans. High taxes—without representation—was only one form of oppression. Cruel punishments, including crucifixion, were meted out daily. All a Roman soldier had to do was order, and a Jew had to carry his baggage for a mile.

But Jesus was aware—and concerned—about another yoke of bondage. The law, the moral precepts God had given his people, had become bogged down in sometimes meaningless ritual and minutia. The people were oppressed not only by the Roman legions but also by some Jewish leaders. Jesus seemed more concerned about money changers and some Pharisees than he was about the Romans.

It must have come as quite a surprise when he offered his followers yet another yoke. And it was an offer he made to those who were already weary and carrying heavy burdens. "Take my yoke," he said, "and you will find rest." What did this mean to the simple peasants and farmers who flocked around him? He was saying that, in contrast to the teaching of the scribes, his way was easy.

The simplicity of his call was truly liberating to those who were willing to listen. And now it is to us, too. This is because the bondage most of us experience is to ourselves. To act in our own interests is complicated. We often find ourselves enmeshed in a web of deception and mistrust. We don't know what to do, and we worry about what others will think.

But as we focus on God and others, we find life is much less stressful. Our choices become clearer, our lives happier. We find the rest our anxious spirits crave. Compared to a life of selfish ambition, or even of Roman occupation, God's way is less wearisome, and his burden is much lighter.

His yoke is easy for another reason, too. It isn't just comparatively easier. It really is just easier. That's because we work willingly for what we love. You might work ten times harder playing basketball or weeding your garden than you do when you're cleaning the house; you don't complain a bit if it's something you love to do.

Jesus isn't saying that following him will be without its difficulties. In fact, in other places he says we might even have a cross of our own to bear. But he is saying that as we experience his gentle and humble heart, we will love him. Then our yoke will be easy and our burdens will be light. And that's a promise.

Depending on You

Remind us, Lord, that you dwell among the lowliest of people. You are the God of the poor, walking with beggars, making your home with the sick and the unemployed. Keep us always mindful that no matter how much we have, our great calling is to depend on you—for everything, every day of our lives.

In the Dark

I know that my character is what I am in the dark when no one is watching and no one can see. Therefore, bless me in my solitude, because temptation is the greatest here and the possibility of a setback looms large.

The Lord is my light and my salvation; whom shall I fear? The Lord is the stronghold of my life; of whom shall I be afraid?

—PSALM 27:1

Lord, either lighten my burden or strengthen my back.

—THOMAS FULLER

*H*ow often we look upon God as
our last and feeblest resource!
We go to him because we have
nowhere else to go. And then we
learn that the storms of life have
driven us, not upon the rocks,
but into the desired haven.

—GEORGE MACDONALD

An Immovable Force

**Cast your burden on the Lord, and he will
sustain you; he will never permit the
righteous to be moved.**
—Psalm 55:22

*T*his verse is a favorite of couch potatoes.
They like the idea that God will never
permit them to be moved. But that's not
exactly what the psalmist had in mind.

Think instead of the elderly couple who
have lived in their home for 50 years. Then the
state highway commission announces it wants
to build a new road—right through their home.
The couple wants to keep their home, but the
commission puts pressure on them, first offer-
ing money, then threats. But the couple stub-
bornly refuse to give up their home, and they
pray for strength to withstand the opposition.
Finally, the road is built elsewhere—they would
not be moved.

Or picture this: UPS delivers a huge box to
your company, and you have to haul it up to
your fifth-floor office. Unfortunately, the eleva-
tors aren't working, so you're carrying it up the
steps. At the fourth-floor landing you start to

totter. Your weary knees are buckling, and you're losing your grip. You're about to take a tumble down four flights with this huge box tumbling right behind you. But then Big Mac shows up, the biggest guy in the mail room. "Here, let me help you with that," he says, and with one sweep of his brawny arms he grabs the box as if it were a child's toy. "You should have let me carry this to begin with."

We often carry burdens that are too big for us. Worries about our future. Guilt about our past. We suffer grief over lost friends and lost opportunities. Sometimes we feel as if we will fall under the weight of all our woes.

But God is there to help us. We can "cast our burdens on the Lord," and he will keep us from falling. Don't let that "righteous" term bother you. Certainly none of us is righteous compared to the Lord. But the psalmist is simply drawing a distinction between those who care about the Lord and those who don't. It's not about having a spotless life—if it were, then no one would have a chance. It's about trusting God to provide comfort in your times of crisis.

So let him carry the things that are weighing you down.

Blessing for This Night

The day has been long, Lord, but that's water under the bridge. Bless me now with stillness and sleep. I sigh and turn over, knowing that night will usher in the day with new joys and possibilities, gifts from your ever-wakeful spirit.

Identity Crisis

See what love the Father has given us,
that we should be called children of God;
and that is what we are.
—1 JOHN 3:1

John and Josie have a daughter, Karin.
They waited a long time to be parents, and
it's obvious they're enjoying it. Their whole
church enjoys watching this family, and it's
delightful to see little Karin resemble her parents more and more as she grows.

It's not unusual to see a child take after his
or her parents. We often comment on children
being "a chip off the old block" or a "spittin'
image" of a parent. As we pass DNA from one
generation to the next, certain physical characteristics are shared. You get your dad's big nose,
your mom's gentle eyes, maybe your grandpa's
potbelly. Interests are also shared, often careers.
Phone books are full of businesses that have
the ending "& Son," and in another generation
we'll have some businesses with the "& Daughter" ending. Kids go fishing with their folks or
attend the theater, establishing habits they'll
carry throughout their lives. We are our par-

ents' progenies, and that determines a great
deal of who we turn out to be.

The thing about John and Josie, though, is
that they adopted little Karin when she was
already 1½. Karin doesn't have their DNA, but
amazingly she still resembles her adoptive
parents, and more so every week.

And that's a picture of our relationship
with God. He has adopted us into his family,
and now we're his children. As we spend more
and more time with him, we become more and
more like him. We share his interests, his values, and his characteristics. We go into his line
of work, helping people, being creative, and
finding others to adopt.

Love makes this happen. God's astounding
love reaches out for us when we have nothing
to offer. He makes us his own children and
pours his love into our hearts. His love trans-
forms us, giving us a new identity.

We live in a time when people are desperately trying to "find themselves." Major maga-
zines run tests where you check off certain
answers, and the tests give you adjectives to
describe your personality. "If you scored 50
to 100, you're polite and easygoing. If 25 to
49, you're mean and surly." Bookstores are
crammed with volumes on self-awareness.

We have colors, seasons, planets, and tempera-
ments to label ourselves. But still we cry, "Who
am I?"

John puts it so simply in 1 John 3:1. As we
accept God's love, we can call ourselves the
children of God. "And that is what we are." We
are adopted through the sacrifice of Jesus into
a new family. We have a new name and a new
nature.

In Romans 8, the apostle Paul discusses
this new life we have. We are to live by God's
Spirit, rejecting our old, selfish desires. But no
longer are we enslaved to fear. We don't behave
ourselves because we're afraid of the consequences of misbehaving. Not anymore. We have
received "the spirit of adoption." We're not
slaves in the household of faith, but beloved
children. We strive to please God with our lives
because that is who we are. The Spirit is constantly whispering to our hearts that we are,
indeed, God's own (Romans 8:15–16).

So rest in that assurance. When you're not
sure who you are or how much you matter,
stop and listen to those divine whispers. God
loves you dearly, as his own child. And that is
what you are.

Overwhelmed?

*A*re insurmountable problems about to do you in? Are you nearly overwhelmed with difficulties, emergencies, and trials of all kinds? These may be divinely appointed instruments for the Holy Spirit to use in your life. It could take days or even weeks, but if you are patient and willing to find out how God plans to use your current struggles, they can become an avenue for spiritual growth. Problems can turn into possibilities. Tribulations can become a blessing that God could get to you in no other way.

Bring all your problems to the Lord. Hold them up to him in prayer. Sit quietly and wait for him to work. Your restless fretting accomplishes nothing. Rest! Wait! Pray! Do nothing that you are not thoroughly convinced in your spirit he is leading you to do. Give God a chance to work. The insurmountable problems that you face today will become God's opportunity to reveal his love and grace to you as you have never known before.

A Roof Over Our Heads

Bless this roof over our heads, and keep it from leaking. But more than that, move us to give thanks for the next rainstorm. Because you are more than a good roof—we need to remember that. And our neighbors' crops need watering more than we need to stay dry.

Blessed are the poor in spirit,
  for theirs is the kingdom of
  heaven.
Blessed are those who mourn,
  for they will be comforted.
Blessed are the meek, for they
  will inherit the earth.
Blessed are those who hunger
  and thirst for righteousness,
  for they will be filled.
Blessed are the merciful, for they
  will be shown mercy.
Blessed are the pure in heart, for
  they will see God.
Blessed are the peacemakers, for
  they will be called the sons
  of God.
Blessed are those who are
  persecuted because of
  righteousness, for theirs is the
  kingdom of heaven.

Blessed are you when people
   insult you, persecute you and
   falsely say all kinds of evil
   against you because of me.
   Rejoice and be glad, because
   great is your reward in heaven.
   —MATTHEW 5:3–12 NIV

The Blessing of Rest

Lord, bless this time of recreation.
May we see that it is much more than
another form of employment. It is a time to
pull back and relax, to honor a thing
you highly value—rest.

Thanksgiving is nothing if not a
   glad and reverent lifting of the
   heart to God in honour and
   praise for His goodness.
   —JAMES R. MILLER

Psalm 23

The Lord is my shepherd, I shall
    not want.
He makes me lie down in green
    pastures;
he leads me beside still waters;
he restores my soul.
He leads me in right paths
for his name's sake.
Even though I walk through the
    darkest valley,

I fear no evil;
for you are with me;
your rod and your staff—they
comfort me.
You prepare a table before me
in the presence of my enemies;
you anoint my head with oil;
my cup overflows.
Surely goodness and mercy shall
follow me
all the days of my life,
and I shall dwell in the house of
the Lord
my whole life long.

*Thank you, Lord, for caring for me
like a shepherd who cares for his sheep.*

Rest and Comfort Under the Shepherd's Care

I don't think I have ever been to a funeral where Psalm 23 was not used. This psalm has given so much comfort to those who are mourning. Yet, if we use this passage only at funerals, we miss the comfort and wisdom that it offers for everyday living.

God is like a shepherd who knows us; he takes care of our needs. That affirmation begins the psalm. Though shepherds worked long and hard, faced many difficulties, and ranked at the lower end of the social scale, we tend to have positive, pastoral images of them.

We are comforted that Jesus called himself a shepherd: "I am the good shepherd. I know my own and my own know me" (John 10:14).

God invites us to rest, whether in green pastures or beside still streams. In our busy society, we often only dream of truly resting. I read a study of office workers that said in a given day they receive or send 177 messages: memos, faxes, e-mails, beepers, phone calls, call forwarding, and even letters. We are more in touch and more overwhelmed than ever before. In the midst of our global village, the psalmist invites us to rest, restore our soul, and find comfort.

We can turn off our pagers, sleep in late, take a walk, smell the flowers, and linger over a meal. We can sit beside a river and listen to the sound of water dancing around the stones. We can look at the trees reaching toward the sky and feel our spirits stretching toward the heavens.

Several times I have come close to burnout. One of the first remedies for burnout is rest. I take some time each day for myself; I take some time each week for really healing and renewing. The Hebrews called it *sabbath*. They took a day to prepare so that on sabbath, they would not have to do work. They could give themselves over to worship, study, prayer, and family. They could take time to restore their souls and refocus their direction. They could remind themselves that God was a shepherd who cared for them, who led them to freedom from captivity, and who walked with them beside still waters.

The psalm shifts from resting to moving. God cares about the directions we are going. God wants to lead us on "right paths," paths of honesty, integrity, kindness, and compassion. Each morning I ask God to guide me through the meetings and events coming that day. I trust the words of the psalm—God wants to lead me.

There are days and events that are dark valleys, and even then the psalmist assures us that God is present. God's presence casts out fear and provides us with comfort. It is these verses that people hold onto in the midst of grief. The King James translation of the Bible calls this the "valley of the shadow of death." All of us walk through that valley at some time in our lives. After a memorial service for a young boy who had drowned, people in our city came up to me and said, "I am really shaken by this tragedy. I can't stop crying, but people in your church seem to be doing better than I am. Why?" People in our church were equally devastated by the death, but they had a faith to see them through; they believed in the words of Psalm 23: "I fear no evil; for you are with me; your rod and your staff—they comfort me." They shed tears, but they knew the comfort of the shepherd.

I believe we shall continue to read Psalm 23 at every funeral, and, I hope, it will be our daily companion as well.

Seek God's Goodness

Let the simple life take you by the hand today, and seek the goodness that only God can put in your heart. Be blessed and warmed in his life-giving presence!

Blessed be the God and Father
of our Lord Jesus Christ, who
has blessed us in Christ with
every spiritual blessing in the
heavenly places.

—Ephesians 1:3

*May the joy and peace
of the Lord fill your soul all
the days of your life.*

With Joy

and

Peace

Joy Goes Beyond Happiness

How wonderful that God wants us to go beyond the pursuit of happiness to experience
joy! We can be joyful even when we're
unhappy.

*A*ll sorts of things can undermine happiness—time, change, and tragedy above
all. There isn't anything intrinsically wrong
with happiness, but trying to build on just the
right set of circumstances is too insecure a
base...

But the answer is not to reject happiness, it
is to go beyond it, to joy.... Joy is different
from happiness because of the cause of the
ultimacy of its fulfillment and because it is a
profound reality regardless of our circumstances. Rooted in God, empowered by the
energies of the resurrection, joy does not
depend on getting the right income, the perfect
spouse, the right mix of things. Joy goes so far
beyond happiness that it is present even in the
midst of deep unhappiness.

—REBECCA MANLEY PIPPERT,
HOPE HAS ITS REASONS

*E*very saint in heaven is as a
flower in the garden of God,
and every soul there is as
a note in some concert of
delightful music.

—JONATHAN EDWARDS

Time to Sing!

*I will sing to the Lord, because he has
dealt bountifully with me.*

Prayer for Joy

*Pressures in our lives can crowd out
the joy. Let's remember to pray and ask
God to help us discover renewed joy.*

The Angel of Peace

Peace I leave with you; my peace I give to you.
I do not give to you as the world gives.
Do not let your hearts be troubled,
and do not let them be afraid.
—JOHN 14:27

These words of Jesus are some of the most comforting in the Bible. Jesus brings us God's peace. It is a different peace than the world gives. It is a deep and lasting peace, no matter what troubles are going on around you. I read these words and feel a great wave of calm wash over me. I am thankful to be in the presence of God—who brings inner peace and outward hope, who settles the troubled heart and dissolves our fears.

The world most often talks about peace as the absence of war. In many countries where there is still fighting and bloodshed, where war still works its destruction, this is a peace that is desired and necessary. It is right to pray and work for an end to killing in these places of violence. It is hard to have any kind of peace as long as people experience the destruction of their lives and property.

Yet, the absence of war does not ensure that there is peace. There can still be hunger, poverty, resentment, bitterness, and distrust that get in the way of living together in peace. Many nations have found building peace and reconciliation as hard as stopping the fighting. One of the first things the new government in South Africa did after the system of discrimination known as apartheid was dismantled was to appoint a minister of reconciliation. The new president knew that the anger and resentments from the past needed to be addressed, so he chose a well-respected bishop to lead the efforts of reconciliation.

The peace that Jesus leaves is deeper than national policy or the absence of war. Jesus brings a peace that not only encompasses the absence of war but also takes up residence inside us. God's peace is an inside job. God's peace is forgiveness for our past mistakes and courage for the future. God's peace keeps our hearts untroubled and unafraid. God's peace gives us a perspective to encounter the world and its violence with a calm and enduring presence. God's peace is the knowledge that we do not face the world alone. We are accompanied by God, within us and all around us.

In our sanctuary, there is a small ceramic angel that sits on our communion table. It just showed up after we'd had a number of funerals in the congregation, including a four-year-old boy who drowned and a 23-year-old man who died of a drug overdose. These deaths deeply affected the community, and, in the midst of the grief, there were also doubts, questions, and anger. How could God let this happen to ones so young and full of life? Where was God? That's when the angel appeared. I don't know who brought it and left it for us, but I like the sense that, in the midst of our grieving, God sent an angel to remind us where to take our questions and who it is that brings us peace.

The angel silently sits there as a testimony to the mysterious yet comforting presence of God. In the midst of sorrow, we seek a deeper peace that will not only get us through the days but also give us the courage to live joyfully, thankfully, and unafraid.

The Hebrew word for peace is *shalom*. The word carries a sense of inner peace and a sense of well-being in the community. It is not only a greeting for individuals, but it also describes the nature of life lived within a community. The Jewish understanding can broaden our understanding of peace to move beyond the individual to incorporate the wider community.

The peace God gives passes all understanding, yet it is experienced by you and me. Celebrate the peace given to us: Shalom!

The Lord blesses
his people with peace.

—PSALM 29:11 (NIV)

Joy

**I have said these things to you
so that my joy may be in you,
and that your joy may be complete.**
—JOHN 15:11

Mike had great news. He had been accepted at the city's college for the performing arts. Now he needed a scholarship so he could afford to go there, and the chances of this looked pretty good. It seemed that he was on his way to a bright new future in which he could use his considerable acting talent. It was a joyous day.

The following weeks piled joy on top of joy. He did get the scholarship and was able to enroll. He started classes a few months later. The curriculum was tough, but Mike worked hard. The students were a bit snobbish at first, but Mike's gentle spirit soon won them over. Recently, he appeared in a school musical—a small role, but he performed well. Joy on top of joy on top of joy.

Good news often comes to us like this, in small pieces. We rejoice over one thing that promises better things. Joy often rides a rough road—hard work, some setbacks—but it's definitely worth the trip.

Jesus had already brought great joy to his disciples. By calling them to follow him, he welcomed them on a wild adventure. They had front-row seats for his teaching, his healings, his squabbles with the religious leaders. They went through storms with Jesus, hungry days and sleepless nights, but they were *living,* perhaps for the first time in their lives. He had announced that his purpose was to give his people life—more than that: *abundant* life, life overflowing. That's what they were enjoying.

But lately Jesus' talk had turned to grimmer subjects. He was headed to Jerusalem, into the teeth of the opposition; he knew he would die there. The disciples were probably so much in denial that they missed his prediction of a joyous resurrection. Now they were in Jerusalem, and here at this Passover supper, Jesus was speaking again about love. The Father loved Jesus, Jesus loved the Father, and they both loved the disciples. Jesus said he was a "vine" and they were all "branches," connected to him, drawing nourishment from him— another one of Jesus' great word pictures.

Why was he saying all this? So that their joy would be complete. Apparently, the wonders of

following Jesus were just the beginning of the
good news. There was another shoe to drop.
They would be spiritually tied with Jesus
through all eternity, loving him and being
loved. The joy of this relationship would lead
them to the cross, to the tomb, and beyond—to
a stunning reunion with the risen Lord. Their
joy would carry them out to the world in min-
istry and ultimately to heaven in triumph.
Their joy would be truly complete.

For modern-day disciples, there is much joy
in pondering Jesus' teachings and watching
him work in people's lives. But our joy begins
to be complete when we connect with him, as a
branch to the vine, tied to him in love.

*T*he Lord bless you and keep
you; the Lord make his face to
shine upon you, and be gracious
to you; the Lord lift up his
countenance upon you,
and give you peace.

—NUMBERS 6:24–26

In a New Place

May God grant that you will find
    happiness in your new destination—
in the transition from country to
    city: peace.
in the move from friends to
    strangers: acceptance.
in the letting go of the old to
    embrace the new: confidence.
in the challenge of new work:
    unflagging zeal.
In all these ways, the blessing of
    God be upon you.

Joy in the Morning

When a woman is in labor, she has pain,
because her hour has come. But when her child
is born, she no longer remembers the anguish
because of the joy of having brought a human
being into the world. So you have your pain
now, but I will see you again, and your hearts
will rejoice, and no one will take
your joy from you.
—JOHN 16:21–22

*L*ike many couples having their children in
the 1970s and 1980s, my wife and I did
the natural childbirth thing. We took Lamaze
classes, and we saw it as a bonding experience.
But we went one step further than our friends—
we had all four of our children with a midwife,
two of them at home.

Although we know many fine, devoted
medical people, Katie felt hospitals intruded
unnecessarily into a natural process. And for a
time she entertained the idea that childbirth
could be painless, even without drugs. That
was before she actually had a baby.

Since I'm the dad and not the mom, I really
have no idea what kind of pain she experienced.

But I do know she worked really hard. That's why they call it labor. She groaned and cried and screamed. She even bit my arm once. And when it was all over, she was physically and emotionally exhausted.

I especially remember our son Michael's birth. Katie had a short but intense labor, about five hours. When he was finally born, about 8:00 in the morning, he was purple. "Breathe, baby, breathe," the midwife said. When he did, we all did. It was a very happy moment.

I held him, and then his sister, who was ten at the time, held him. Then we dressed him and put him into the cradle. Katie was too exhausted even to pick him up. But later that morning, after we all had recovered, she held him and nursed him. Once we put that baby in her arms, she didn't for a moment resent the effort it took to get him here.

Her mom was there and so was her sister. That evening, I took the kids out into the yard, and we set off some fireworks. We had a loud and joyous celebration, and we praised God for a new and healthy boy. It was certainly worth the work. Just to look at him made our hearts pound with excitement and gratitude.

Christ said the joy we will experience when he returns will be something like that. Our work to extend his kingdom in the world will be rewarded. Our hearts will rejoice, and no one will be able to take away our joy. That should be a loud and joyous celebration, too, and one that will last for a very long time.

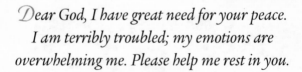

Dear God, I have great need for your peace. I am terribly troubled; my emotions are overwhelming me. Please help me rest in you.

*J*oy is not the same as pleasure or happiness. A wicked and evil man may have pleasure, while any ordinary mortal is capable of being happy. Pleasure generally comes from things, and always through the senses; happiness comes from humans through fellowship. Joy comes from loving God and neighbor. Pleasure is quick and violent, like a flash of lightning. Joy is steady and abiding, like a fixed star. Pleasure depends on external circumstances, such as money, food, travel, etc. Joy is independent of them, for it comes from a good conscience and love of God.

—BISHOP FULTON J. SHEEN

Add Brightness

*B*ritish Bible scholar William Barclay had to chuckle when he saw a detergent ad with only two words: Adds brightness! "I don't know if there could be a better definition of the effect of the Christian life," he commented. "If a person is a true Christian, he or she will add brightness everywhere."

Suzy is a person like that. When she agreed to play piano for a brand-new church, she didn't know what she was getting into. Her regular involvement with the church deepened her relationship with God, and that ignited her joyous heart. Whenever she played or sang or talked she overflowed with joy. It was contagious. The church's music was upbeat and down-to-earth; it came from hearts that were excited about the Lord. The whole church became a place where people enjoyed themselves, enjoyed one another, and rejoiced in God.

Not that everything was hunky-dory all the time. As Suzy grew in her faith, she realized she had to break up with a boyfriend who felt threatened by her newfound fervor. That was difficult. Later there were health problems in her family that caused her great concern. But joy isn't built on the ups and downs of our lives, it's based on our relationship with God. No matter the circumstances, God is constant, showing us love and energizing our hearts. As Suzy keeps connecting with him, her life radiates with an exultant joy.

Maybe you're not as bubbly as Suzy, but God promises to bring joy to your life, too. It could be a big celebration or a quiet satisfaction, but it's rooted in the amazing goodness of our loving Lord.

*B*e kind to your little children, Lord. Be a gentle teacher, patience with our weakness and stupidity. And give us the strength and discernment to do what you tell us, and so grow in your likeness. May we all live in the peace that comes from you. May we journey towards your city, sailing through the waters of sin untouched by the waves, borne serenely along by the Holy Spirit. Night and day may we give you praise and thanks, because you have shown us that all things belong to you, and all blessings are gifts from you. To you, the essence of wisdom, the foundation of truth, be glory for evermore.

—CLEMENT OF ALEXANDRIA, *TO THE DIVINE TUTOR*

Like a River Glorious

Like a river glorious is God's
    perfect peace,
over all victorious in its bright
    increase;
perfect, yet it floweth fuller
    every day,
perfect, yet it groweth deeper
    all the way.
Ev'ry joy or trial falleth from
    above,
traced upon our dial by the
    sun of love;
we may trust him fuller all for
    us to do—
they who trust him wholly find
    him wholly true.
Stayed upon Jehovah, hearts are
    fully blest—
finding, as he promised, perfect
    peace and rest.

—FRANCES RIDLEY HAVERGALE

But all who humble themselves
before the Lord shall be given
every blessing, and shall have
wonderful peace.

—PSALM 37:11 (TLB)

When Laughter Fades

*O*ne of the worst things about my ten-
month-old's sickness, which the doctors
called "failure to thrive" and which led to weeks
in the hospital, was when she reached a point
where she did not laugh. Before she got sick,
she loved to repeatedly cover and uncover her
eyes and laugh heartily every time I said, "Peek-
aboo." Often I'd tickle her tummy and say,
"Coochie coochie coo," as she laughed glee-
fully. I tried these when she was in the hospital.
It broke my heart that she would not, could
not, laugh or even smile.

I recall the day I prayed, telling God how
much I missed her laughter. I then went up to
her room, and for the first time in days, she
played all the little games, and she laughed and
laughed. It was like medicine to my soul. The
next day, the laughter disappeared again, but it
was enough to help me through the rest of her
illness. She is a healthy teen now, and I still love
to hear the sound of her laughter.

I wonder, does God love to hear the sound
of our laughter? Does it break his heart when
we are no longer able or willing to laugh? Does
it lift him up when we resume our laughter?
The answer to these questions is "Yes."

With Acceptance Comes Peace

We can decide to be at peace with the state of our lives. If we're constantly desiring more and better things and positions, rather than being contented with what we have, we'll never know true peace.

To enjoy a little happiness, to have a taste of heaven on earth, you must accept life, your own life, just as it is now. You must be at peace with your work, with the people around you, with their faults and their imperfections. You must be content with your husband or your wife, even if you now realize you did not marry the ideal husband or the ideal wife. (I don't believe they exist anyway.) You must be at peace with the size of your purse, your status in the community, with your face (which you did not choose yourself), with your home, your furniture, your clothes, with your own living standards—even if your neighbors' things are so much better and so much finer, so you think. Accept life. You only have one skin. You can't be born again in another one.

—PHIL BOSMANS, *GIVE HAPPINESS A CHANCE*

Blessings of Wisdom

Blessings upon you.
The blessing of perfect
acceptance in the face of
daunting circumstances.
The blessing of contentment and
peace while the winds blow
and the waves rise higher and
higher.

Blessings upon you.
The blessing of knowing when
 acceptance must turn to
 action for the sake of all
 concerned.
The blessing of strength to
 forsake contentment and
 peace for the purpose of
 comforting another.
Blessings upon you.
The blessing of discernment: to
 recognize when to wait, and to
 understand when to move.

*W*eeping may endure
for a night, but joy cometh
in the morning.
—Psalm 30:5 (KJV)

In Heaven Above

In heav'n above, in heav'n above,
where God our Father dwells,
how boundless there the
   blessedness!
No tongue its greatness tells.
There face to face, and full
   and free,
the ever living God we see—
our God, the Lord of hosts!
In heav'n above, in heav'n above,
what glory deep and bright!
The splendor of the noon-
   day sun
grows pale before its light:
The heav'nly light that ne'er goes
   down,
around whose radiance clouds
   ne'er frown,
is God, the Lord of hosts!

In heav'n above, in heav'n above,
no tears of pain are shed,
for nothing there can fade
   or die—
life's fullness round is spread;
and, like an ocean, joy o'er flows,
and with immortal mercy glows
our God, the Lord of hosts!
In heav'n above, in heav'n above,
God has a joy prepared
which mortal ear has never heard
nor mortal vision shared,
which ever entered mortal
   breast,
by mortal lips was n'er expressed:
'tis God, the Lord of hosts!

—LAURENTIUS L. LAURINUS, ALT.,
JOHN ASTROM, TRANSLATED BY
WILLIAM MACCALL

*W*e—or at least I—shall not be
able to adore God on the highest
occasions if we have learned no
habit of doing so on the lowest.
At best, our faith and reason will
tell us that He is adorable, but
we shall not have found Him so,
not have "tasted and seen."
Any patch of sunlight in a wood
will show you something about
the sun which you could never
get from reading books on
astronomy. These pure and
spontaneous pleasures are
"patches of Godlight" in the
woods of our experience.

—C. S. LEWIS, *THE QUOTABLE LEWIS:*
LETTERS TO MALCOM: CHIEFLY ON PRAYER

I will praise the Lord
as long as I live.

—Psalm 146:2

*M*usical theater can seem unrealistic. If you've watched *Oklahoma!* or *The Sound of Music* or *The King and I* on stage or at the movies, you know what I'm talking about. Two people are chatting away, and suddenly one bursts into song. Imagine if that happened in real life. You're pushing your cart through the supermarket and suddenly the music begins and the cashiers start belting out, "Will you buy our cabbages? Mushrooms and radishes?"

You might look for another place to shop.

I used to make fun of musicals until I realized what they're about. Musicals heighten the emotions of characters until they just have to sing. When you feel deeply about something, mere words aren't enough. You must burst into song. Granted, some musicals are pretty corny about this, but they've created a world in which emotions are naturally expressed in music and in song.

Is that so strange?

Sometimes you're so happy that you probably find yourself humming or whistling a tune. If you're in the shower where no one can hear you (you hope), you may even perform a concert. If you're in the car with the radio blasting, you may sing along. Even if you're not a singer, you may drum your fingers, clap your hands, or take a few impromptu dance steps during times of high emotion.

That's where the psalmist finds himself when he writes his psalm (see Psalm 13). He has to sing because the Lord has dealt bountifully with him. As Paul said in Ephesians 3:20, the Lord "by the power at work within us is able to accomplish abundantly far more than all we can ask or imagine." That's enough to make you want to sing.

*I love the Lord,
because he has heard my voice
and my supplications.
Because he inclined his ear to
me, therefore I will call on
him as long as I live.*

—Psalm 116:1–2

The Blessings
of Prayer

A Dad and His Lad

My wife was the seventh of ten kids, and she could barely get a word in edgewise. Even if she could, I doubt it would matter much. In some ways her grandparents' strict "children should be seen and not heard" philosophy permeated her Michigan home.

On the other hand, I'm from the South, a fifth-generation Floridian, and we were much more laid back. So Katie had reason to think I was spoiled, and she was right. A firstborn son with two much-younger sisters, I had—at least when she first met me—the mistaken notion that the planet revolved around my head.

One of the things she found most irritating was my tendency to interrupt people when they were talking, especially older adults. My dad is a pastor. He would be talking to parishioners, and I would walk up to him, ask him a question, and then go on my merry way. I'm not sure which she found more annoying—that I would do it or that he would let me.

But one thing I experienced almost all my life was unrestricted access to my dad. I wasn't allowed to monopolize a conversation, but I could ask a question or make a request at almost any time. And while he may not have been teaching me about good manners, he was teaching me something about prayer.

You see, for years my wife had trouble praying or at least believing that God was paying any attention to her. But I always felt as though he was right there, interested in what I had to say and what I needed.

To some degree, all of us understand who God is and how he works in terms of our own fathers. He is often called Father in the Scriptures, of course, but the New Testament even refers to him with the more familiar Aramaic term *abba,* which means something like "daddy."

I feel fortunate that, at least in this regard, I got the right picture. God is interested in us and what we have to say. The psalmist describes it this way: "On the day I called, you answered me, you increased my strength of soul" (Psalm 138:3).

The Bible promises us access to God's throne, not as a subject, but as a child. It reminds me of a story I heard about Abraham Lincoln. When his young son Tad interrupted a war cabinet meeting in the White House, the president was scolded by one of his generals.

"It's really no bother," Lincoln replied. "This is my son."

I'm glad God feels the same way about me, and about you.

Pray With Patience

Should you, however, not at once obtain answers to your prayers, be not discouraged; but continue patiently, believingly, persever-ingly to wait upon God: and as assuredly as that which you ask would be for your real good, and therefore for the honor of the Lord; and as assuredly as you ask it solely on the ground of the worthiness of the Lord Jesus, so assuredly you will at last obtain the blessing. I myself have had to wait upon God concerning certain matters for years, before I obtained answers to my prayers; but at last they came.

—GEORGE MULLER

Maintaining Integrity

This excerpt from a letter dated July 17, 1861, is from a father to his only son, an infantry soldier during the Civil War.

Try to maintain your Christian profession among your comrades. I need not caution you against strong drink as useless and hurtful, nor against profanity, so common among soldiers. Both these practices you abhor. Aim to take at once a decided stand for God. If practicable have prayers regularly in your tent, or unite with fellow-disciples in prayer-meetings in the camp. Should preaching be accessible, always be a hearer. Let the world know that you are a Christian. Read a chapter in the New Testament, which your mother gave you, every morning and evening, when you can, and engage in secret prayer to God for his holy Spirit to guide and sustain you.

—FROM *SOLDIER LIFE*
BY CARLTON MCCARTHY

Navigating Life's Rapids

*L*ike canoeists on the river rapids, O God,
we learn that there is an easy way and a
hard way to get through life. Our days are as
tumultuous as any rock-strewn river, and life is
as frightening as an unstable canoe:

Work—too much or too little. Age—too old
or too young. Family—too near or too far. Too
little time and money but too much demand.
Meanness and violence making us hostages to
fear. Stress, tragedy. Shifting values. A rock-
strewn life.

It takes a guide and a cheering family to
make it through both life and river rapids. The
hard way, as you remind us, is alone. Cut off
from you, cut off from others, we miss the
abundant life you promise. Yet running life's
course as your child is as life-changing as riding
river rapids. Both require moving into uncer-
tain waters, taking a chance on a guide we can't
see, and listening for the encouragement of
those we can.

Come, God of wanderers and pilgrims, be
our companion and guide. Let prayer be a
bridge, a meeting place spanning icy floodwa-

ters. We sense you near and are grateful to no longer be alone, knowing that choosing to live relying on you as our guide is a move as major as paddling onto the deepest, wildest river.

Steady us, for faith, like white-water rafting, isn't for cowards. It is a leap, a bold intention to become forever changed by showing our trust in you. It is a loud, resounding "Yes!" to your invitation: *Come, get in the boat, be fishers of folk, teach, preach, heal; be my child . . . I will guide and go with you so you don't have to flounder alone.*

Accepting it, we know that you will be first there when we tip and that we need only listen to hear your directions. We feel excitement building as we antici-pate the journey. There's an easy way and a hard way to do river rapids. To do life. With you, O God, as guide, we joyfully move into the swift currents of life. Amen.

If You Need Wisdom, Ask God

*I*f any of you need wisdom, you
should ask God, and it will be
given to you. God is generous
and won't correct you for asking.
But when you ask for something,
you must have faith
and not doubt.

—JAMES 1:5-6, *THE PROMISE*

Prayer Brings Peace

*I*nstead of lugging around our cares, we can
pray. Prayer opens the door to peace.

*Lord, I appreciate all the work you went
through to make me your child, and
I'm willing to serve because I know I will see
you later. I claim both now and then
your everlasting joy. Amen*

"Most of us don't pray on a regular basis because we're deeply aware that it will cost us something. More than time. More than money. More than faith. More than becoming religious. To lay hold of prayer as my own available resource for effective, practical, daily use—as an abiding certainty in an unpredictable world—will cost me one thing. *Honesty*."

—JACK W. HAYFORD,
PRAYER IS INVADING THE IMPOSSIBLE

Best Friend

Know this: Prayer is quite informal, one heart communing with another, with or without words. If we make it any more complicated than that, have we not insulted our very best Friend?

Sweet Hour of Prayer

Sweet hour of prayer,
sweet hour of prayer,
that calls me from a world of care,
and bids me at my Father's throne
make all my wants and wishes
    known.
In seasons of distress and grief
my soul has often found relief,
and oft escaped the tempter's snare,
by thy return, sweet hour of prayer.
Sweet hour of prayer,
sweet hour of prayer,
the joy I feel, the bliss I share,
of those whose anxious spirits burn
with strong desires for thy return!
Sweet hour of prayer,
sweet hour of prayer,
thy wings shall my petition bear
to him whose truth and faithfulness
engage the waiting soul to bless.

And since he bids me seek his face,
believe his Word, and trust his grace,
I'll cast on him my ev'ry care,
and wait for thee, sweet hour of
    prayer.

—WILLIAM WALFORD

Lord,
I'm glad that you picked the spot
where I can pray. Please show it to me today
so I can enjoy your presence. Amen.

God answers sharp and sudden
   on some prayers.
And thrusts the thing we have
   prayed for in our face,
A gauntlet with a gift in't.

—ELIZABETH BARRETT BROWNING,
"AURORA LEIGH"

A Prayer
by George Washington

Throughout the ages, men who've held the
United States' highest office have gathered
wisdom from the highest authority of all.
George Washington (1732–1799), the first
President of the United States, once said, "I
now make my earnest prayer that God would
be most graciously pleased to dispose us all to
do justice, to love mercy, and to demean ourselves with that charity, humility, and pacific
temper of mind which were the characteristics
of the divine Author of our blessed religion."

*P*rayer is one of the privileges of
the child of God, made possible
because Jesus Christ has opened
up the way to our Father. God
loves you, and He wants you to
"not be anxious about anything,
but in everything, by prayer and
petition, with thanksgiving,
present your request to God"
(Philippians 4:6).

—BILLY GRAHAM,
ANSWERS TO LIFE'S PROBLEMS

People of God

*C*oming together in worship with prayer,
song, and psalm makes us expectant people.
Here we find what we came seeking: your
abiding, ever-present daily love.
We leave, blessed with the truth that it goes
with us into the rest of our lives.

A Prayer for Humility

Only a life of prayer can help the believer achieve a spirit of humility, meekness, and Christlikeness.

> I am praying, blessed Savior,
> To be more and more like thee;
> I am praying that thy Spirit
> Like a dove may rest on me.
> I am praying, blessed Savior,

For a faith so clear and bright
That its eye will see thy glory
Thro' the deepest, darkest night.
I am praying to be humbled
By the power of grace divine,
To be clothed upon with
    meekness,
And to have no will but thine.
I am praying, blessed Savior,
And my constant prayer shall be
For a perfect consecration,
That shall make me more like
    thee.

Chorus:
Thou who knowest all my
    weakness,
Thou who knowest all my care,
While I plead each precious
    promise,
Hear, oh, hear and answer prayer.

—FANNY J. CROSBY

Take Heart, Be Hopeful

A friend of mine wrote a song called "Be Brave."

My friend has a big strong voice, and when he sings, I feel tears come to my eyes. I feel wonderfully hopeful and encouraged. I love the song; he mixes individual bravery and a "light" that comes from outside and shines on us. Some days I feel strong and look forward to facing the world, but other days I have to count on a courage that comes from beyond me.

In Psalm 31:24, the psalmist likewise told the Hebrews to keep their focus on the Lord, a strength beyond themselves. The psalmist recognized that the people have a strength that can be encouraged, but he ended the psalm with the deeper strength of the Lord.

There is another biblical passage that talks about "taking heart," of having courage in the circumstances of life. Jesus and his disciples are moving through Jericho when a blind beggar yells out, "Jesus, Son of David, have mercy on me" (Mark 10:47). He yells again, even though people are trying to shut him up. Jesus says, "Call him here." The crowd turns to the beggar and says, "Take heart; get up, he is calling you."

So the man gets up, leaves his begging cloak behind, goes to Jesus, and is healed. The words of the psalmist echo through this passage. The people who have been waiting and hoping—have been strong—are invited to rise up and come to Jesus, who brings healing and hope.

To be strong may not be a matter of physical strength but rather an orientation toward God, who gives us incredible courage in the face of a world that is often filled with fear and violence. To be strong is to know that Jesus is calling, that God is coming, and that hope rests in God.

I begin my mornings with a time of prayer and meditation, a time of waiting on the Lord. I pray for God's presence, asking for courage, and, because God promises to be with me in all circumstances, I have hope. I can go through each day hopeful and with confidence that God will guide me, help me, support me, and challenge me.

Recently a woman asked if she could write a play for our church. She showed me some of her other writing, and I said "yes." When she brought me a script, it did not fit our needs. I worried how to tell her. I did not feel strong-hearted, but in my morning time I asked God for courage. I hoped my meeting with the author would be blessed. It turned out she was glad for more direction. She had been cautious in her first attempt, and she was eager to do better.

Be strong, let your heart take courage, and trust in the Lord.

*D*on't worry about anything;
instead, pray about everything;
tell God your needs and don't
forget to thank him for his
answers. If you do this you will
experience God's peace, which is
far more wonderful than the
human mind can understand.
His peace will keep your
thoughts and your hearts quiet
and at rest as you trust
in Christ Jesus.

—PHILIPPIANS 4:6–7 (TLB)

When People Pray

There's nothing extraordinary about this handful of Christians who meet Tuesday nights for Bible study and prayer. Marian is new to the Christian faith, drinking it all in with gusto. Janet grew up in a Christian home, but she is just now awakening to the idea of applying her faith to her daily life. Lisa is a leader in the church who has been going through hard times. Arnie has a learning disability, but he goes through life with the mischievous grin of a 12-year-old boy.

And lately they've been learning a lot about prayer.

As they've swapped prayer requests, Arnie has reported that he doesn't get along with his boss. Janet has said she feels used and unappreciated in her job as a nurse. Marian announced months ago that she was awaiting a liver transplant that could restore her health. Lisa has often shared her frustrations about her elderly mother, who is losing her health and sanity but refuses to move to a nursing home.

Week by week they prayed for one another. And one day Arnie announced he was offered a new job in the same company, with a nicer boss. Soon Janet said she had a whole new attitude at work, and things turned around for her. God was answering their prayers! But weeks turned to months for Marian, and still no liver was available for transplant. And Lisa's mom just kept getting worse.

One Tuesday, Marian was especially distressed. Her doctor had argued with the hospital, and it seemed the transplant wouldn't happen until it was too late for her. The group prayed that the medical people would act with wisdom. The same night Lisa told of an accident with her mother, who had collapsed at home but still refused to move to a nursing facility. The group prayed for healing for the mother and strength for Lisa in the tough decisions she faced.

The next day Marian got a call from the hospital. "The transplant is ready. Get here now!" She did, and the surgery was successful.

The day after that, Lisa's mother had to be rushed to the hospital with breathing problems. Within a week she had passed away with a minimum of pain, surrounded by her loved ones.

As Lisa prepared to give the eulogy at her mom's funeral, she called the rest of the group to ask for prayer. "You're batting a thousand so far," she quipped. "It's kind of scary, isn't it?"

Absolutely. The power of God is awesome, and his desire to hear our needs and meet them is astounding. We can't always channel his power in precise ways. Sometimes he surprises us with an unexpected change in circumstance—as he did with Arnie, giving him a new, better job. Sometimes he changes us—as he did with Janet, giving her a positive new attitude. Sometimes we have to wait a long time—like Marian—and just when things look bleakest, he comes through for us. And sometimes he answers in strange ways—taking Lisa's mother to her eternal home rather than a nursing home.

There's nothing extraordinary about this group. You could be a part of it. Week by week they're learning to pray—and to trust that God will answer. Such are the blessings of praying to God about our needs and hopes.

All our opportunities, abilities, and resources come from God, our Creator. They are given to us to hold in sacred trust for him. Cooperating with God will permit us to generously pass on to others some of the many blessings from his rich storehouse.

Our Mighty
Healer and
Creator

This Is My Father's World

This is my Father's world,
and to my list'ning ears
all nature sings and round
   me rings
the music of the spheres.
This is my Father's world;
I rest me in the thought
of rocks and trees, of skies
   and seas—
his hand the wonders wrought.
This is my Father's world:
God shines in all that's fair;
in rustling grass I hear
   him pass—
he speaks to me everywhere.
This is my Father's world:
Why should my heart be sad?
The Lord is King,
let heaven ring!
God reigns; let earth be glad.

—MALTBIE BABCOCK
(PRONOUNS HAVE BEEN MODERNIZED)

What Is

Today may you come to acceptance. What is, is. May you find blessed relief in seeing— without judging, being—without having to become, knowing—without needing to change a thing. Then, should you be healed, it will be a gracious, unexpected surprise. May you soon arrive at perfect acceptance.

If you will listen carefully to the
voice of the Lord your God, and
do what is right in his sight, and
give heed to his commandments
and keep all his statutes,
I will not bring upon you any
of the diseases that I brought
upon the Egyptians; for I am the
Lord who heals you.

—Exodus 15:26

Over mountains
and over valleys
and over oceans
and over rivers
and over deserts
one says: Blessed are You, Lord,
    our God, king of the world,
    who makes the works of
    creation…
Over rain
and over good news
one says: Blessed are You, Lord,
    our God, ruler of the world,
    who is God and who does
    good things.
And for bad news
one says: Blessed are You, Lord,
    our God, ruler of the world,
    who is the true judge.

—THE TALMUD, BLESSINGS,
    BERAKHOT 9:2

Heal me, O Lord, and I shall be healed; save me, and I shall be saved; for you are my praise.

—JEREMIAH 17:14

A Night of Blessing

**Bless the Lord, O my soul,
and do not forget all his benefits—
who forgives all your iniquity,
who heals all your diseases.**
—PSALM 103:2–3

*T*wo of humanity's greatest concerns are
addressed in these wonderful verses from
this powerful psalm of thanksgiving—sin and
illness. God is involved in forgiving our mistakes, our sins, our errors. God is actively working to heal our wounds, our illnesses, our
diseases. The poet reminds us not to forget the
many ways God is touching our lives, bringing
us many benefits. Above all, do not forget to
thank God for these kindnesses.

I experienced the weaving of blessing and
healing in a powerful way at a men's retreat.
One evening we were given a strip of red tape
and instructed to go off by ourselves and reflect
on the wounds that we as men had experienced. They could be physical or emotional
wounds we had received. As we remembered
the wounds, we were to put a piece of red tape
on the spot of the wound. As we gathered back

in the candlelit room, we were divided into groups of ten and invited to sit on the floor. Each man was decorated with red pieces of tape. All of us were carrying wounds from life. The leaders invited us to think of words that we wished we had heard from our fathers when we were born, words of blessing and encouragement. We were then instructed to go around the entire circle and whisper those words to each man.

In the darkened room, sitting there conscious of my past, my wounds, I heard nine blessings whispered to me. "I am glad you are here. May you be filled with joy and courage." "I love you and pray you will follow your dreams." "I am here for you. I will take time with you." It was an incredibly healing night to receive these blessings and to be able to give my blessing to others. There were tears shed in that small group. And when the last person finished giving his blessing, we all just sat there, not wanting to move or to let go of the moment. We took off the red pieces of tape and felt whole, forgiven, and healed.

I learned a lot about the importance of giving blessings that night. I learned a lot about healing. I learned about the importance of rituals that let us acknowledge the past and open us to receive forgiveness or healing. I remembered these verses from Psalm 103 and hoped I would not forget the way that our Great Healer works through others to bring about forgiveness and healing.

*H*ave you not known? Have you not heard? The Lord is the everlasting God, the Creator of the ends of the earth. He does not faint or grow weary; his understanding is unsearchable. He gives power to the faint, and strengthens the powerless. Even youths will faint and be weary, and the young will fall exhausted; but those who wait for the Lord shall renew their strength, they shall mount up with wings like eagles, they shall run and not be weary, they shall walk and not faint.

—ISAIAH 40:28–31

The Creator Within

*B*lessed is the one who can look upward and recognize divine glory in the sun and clouds, who can look downward and be moved to praise by stones and flowers. Blessed is the one who can look inside and find the Creator within us, knowing we are never alone, certain there is more to be known than to be seen.

Hide and Seek

**And those who know your name put their
trust in you, for you, O Lord, have not
forsaken those who seek you.
—Psalm 9:10**

*E*ver play hide and seek as a kid? You know,
where the other kids counted to 100 while
you found the best secret spot, then they came
hunting for you? But what if your hiding place
was too good? What if they looked and looked
but could not find you? Well, probably you'd
help them out a little. You'd cough or sneeze to
give them a clue, to keep them in the game. Or
else you'd burst out of your hiding place crow-
ing victory. Yes, the whole point is to find a
good hiding place, but eventually you want to
be found.

People often play hide and seek with God.
It started in the Garden of Eden, when Adam
and Eve sinned and then hid from God because
they were ashamed. We've been playing that
game ever since. There are many times when
we'd prefer not to be found by him. We've got
our own thing happening, and we know God
will just make us feel guilty. So we pretend he's

not there. We say we believe in God, but we live as if we don't.

The wonderful news of the Bible is that *God seeks us.* He wants to be with us, and he'll keep hunting for us. Many Christians today are former hiders; they are living proof of the tenacity of God.

Yet sometimes it seems as if God is hiding from people. The Creator can appear to be distant. When things aren't going well, we might think he doesn't care about us. When blinded by tragedy, we might fear that he's abandoned us.

The psalmist, however, assures us that our Creator won't stay hidden for long. He wants us to find him. Any minute now, he'll burst out of his hiding place. "See, I was here all along!" He does not forsake those who seek him.

Our world is full of spiritual seekers. The materialism of past decades has yielded a generation of folks who know there must be something more to life than wealth and pleasure. Today's verse is great news for these people. The living God is there for you, and he will be found, as long as you keep searching.

Different Is Lovely

*We want to belong and go to great lengths to
fit in anonymously, forgetting we are like
snowflakes, no two, thank God, alike. Each
snowflake and child of yours is the same in
essence but different in form. Bless our unique,
one-of-a-kind value. We are heartened to know
that no one is created more special.
It is not your way as the Creator of all
things to be unnatural, to make one
snowflake better than another.*

Turning to God's Love

They who have my commandments and keep them are those who love me, and those who love me will be loved by my Father, and I will love them and reveal myself to them.
—JOHN 14:21

*S*omeone once wrote, "God loves more than you and before you." Love is the defining characteristic of God. God's love is first; it is primary. We cannot get up early and beat God to loving. There is no place we can travel and not find God's love already present. God's very nature is love.

Douglas Steere, a wonderful Quaker teacher and writer, liked to say that God is forever wooing us and besieging us with love. It is a startling image to think that God is wooing us like a lover, passionately seeking us and yearning for our response. Not only is God's very nature that of love, but God's activities are of love—and the focus of his love is us. God wants us to respond to the courting. We will not find our true home until we turn and respond to the love of God.

The Bible is full of stories of God's love. It begins with creation; God created a world of beauty to call our attention to the Master Designer. God created humans with love, forming them in his own image and filling them with his own breath. We were kissed into being, given eyes to see the wonders of creation and hearts to know that we are connected to the heart of God.

When we turned away, forgot our Maker, and became captives in Egypt, God sent Moses to lead us to freedom and remind us of the great love of God. The story of the Exodus from Egypt has continued to be a shaping story that tells us of the great love of God. Many of the psalms are songs telling that story of redemption. "[The Lord] made known his ways to Moses, his acts to the people of Israel. The Lord is merciful and gracious, slow to anger and abounding in steadfast love" (Psalm 103:7–8).

In the New Testament, we meet Jesus, who is the clearest picture of God's love. God was willing to send his Son that we might see how great his love is. The wooing of the Creator is personal, and we get an incredible picture of God's love by the stories that Jesus told. Perhaps no story gives a better picture than the parable of the waiting father and prodigal son.

Though the son wanders off to spend his inheritance, still the father longs for the son. The father runs to greet the wayward child on his return. The welcome becomes a party and the relationship of child to parent is strengthened and deepened (Luke 15:11–32).

In our verse from John 14, the meeting between God and humanity has occurred. The followers of Jesus have experienced the beckoning love of God and have turned toward it. As they enter into that love, they are given instructions on how to deepen the relationship. The instructions are Jesus' commandments to "Love your God with all your heart, and with all your soul, and with all your mind, and with all your strength" and "You shall love your neighbor as yourself" (Mark 12:30–31).

Jesus says that those who live these commandments will find themselves in constant communion with their Creator, and more of the love of God will be revealed to them. That is a promise.

As pants the deer for the
   cooling streams
when heated in the chase,
so longs my soul, O God,
   for you,
and your refreshing grace.
I sigh to think of happier days
when you, O Lord, were nigh;
when ev'ry heart was tuned
   to praise,
and none more blest than I.
Why restless, why cast down,
   my soul?
Hope still, and you will sing
the praise of him who is
   your God,
your health's eternal spring.

—TATE AND BRADY, HENRY F. LYTE,
   BASED ON PSALM 42, ADAPTED

Healing Memories

How blessed are the good memories, Lord! In fact, I am beginning to see that my happiness can consist largely in the looking back. For that I am thankful to my Healer while I lie here.

Body and Soul

*May you be healed in mind, body, and soul.
May you come to know that all healing
proceeds from God, and he cares about every
part of you. Perhaps the healing will come
sooner for your attitude than for your body.
Perhaps your mind will experience peace
quicker than bones and muscles. But sooner or
later, all will be well.*

How good it is to sing praises to our God,
how pleasant and fitting to praise him!
He heals the brokenhearted
and binds up their wounds.
He determines the number of the stars
and calls them each by name.
Great is our Lord and mighty in power;
his understanding has no limit.
Sing to the Lord with thanksgiving;
make music to our God on the harp.

—Psalm 147:1, 3–5, 7 (NIV)

The Blessing of His Sunshine

*H*eadlines tell a dark sorry tale, God, and depress us about money problems, strife, drugs, and school problems; about housing, wildlife, family, and health problems. Trouble is so news-making we forget the rest of the story. We need sunshine to bring it to light. Send the sun's light through creation: surf and skyline merging, bird song and flight. Send it through people: Friends who laugh at our jokes and family who never stray. Send it through inner knowing: unexplained peace and joy, faith that you're working alongside us. Reading between the lines of the gloom-and-doom true stories, Lord, we celebrate *your* truth and stretch tall with gladness in the sunshine of your creation.

A Blessing for Healers

*B*less those who tend to us when we are ailing. They are a gift from you, Great Healer. Sustain them as they sustain us, for they are a channel of your love.

Steps for Growing in Faith

If we want to grow in faith, we must cooperate
with God. Doing our part is the key to growing
in faith. Getting to know him and his ways will
enable us to "see" what he is asking us to do.

*A*s you know him better, he will give you,
through his great power, everything you
need for living a truly good life: he even shares
his own glory and his own goodness with us!
And by that same mighty power he has given us
all the other rich and wonderful blessings he
promised; for instance, the promise to save us
from the lust and rottenness all around us, and
to give us his own character.

But to obtain these gifts, you need more
than faith; you must also work hard to be
good, and even that is not enough. For then
you must learn to know God better and discover what he wants you to do. Next, learn to
put aside your own desires so that you will
become patient and godly, gladly letting God
have his way with you. This will make possible
the next step, which is for you to enjoy other
people and to like them, and finally you will
grow to love them deeply. The more you go on

in this way, the more you will grow strong spiritually and become fruitful and useful to our Lord Jesus Christ. But anyone who fails to go after these additions to faith is blind indeed, or at least very shortsighted, and has forgotten that God delivered him from the old life of sin so that now he can live a strong, good life for the Lord.

—2 Peter 1:3–9 (TLB)

Lord, Let Me See

Jesus stood still and ordered the man to be
brought to him; and when he came near, he
asked him, "What do you want me to do for
you?" He said, "Lord, let me see again." Jesus
said to him; "Receive your sight; your faith has
saved you." Immediately he regained his sight
and followed him, glorifying God; and all the
people, when they saw it, praised God.
—LUKE 18:40–43

The man in this story, being physically
blind, was unable to see the cause of the
commotion and questioned those around
him. "Jesus of Nazareth is passing by," he was
informed. The blind man, recognizing Jesus
as the Christ, the Anointed One, the Son of
David, added his voice to the crowd. And Jesus
paused in his journey.

Was it the man's shouting or the man's
believing that brought the journey to a halt?
Did Jesus pause in his travels because of the
presence of the crowd or the presence of such
great faith? In the direct encounter between
the two men, Jesus asked the man what he
wanted, for clearly the man already possessed

the ability to see beyond the physical to the spiritual reality. When he asked for his sight, Jesus, the Divine Physician, granted his request. Having his physical sight allowed the man to carry out what his faith had prepared him for—to follow Jesus.

A Blessing for the Earth

*B*less the soil beneath our feet, the sky overhead, and help us be truly concerned about your creation. We are catching on, catching up with ourselves, Creator God, while smelling the garbage around us. Catching, too, a glimpse of the fading streams and trash-strewn seas we have long ignored.

Bless and use our reclamation efforts, for it is a task we can't accomplish alone. With your help, we can bind up and reclaim this poor old earth. We feel whispers of hope in the winds of changed hearts and minds, for we recall your promise to make all things new—even this earth we shall yet learn to tend. We are grateful for another chance.

How precious is your steadfast love, O God! All people may take refuge in the shadows of your wings.

—Psalm 36:7

The Blessings
of God's Love

A Heavenly Honeymoon

"In my father's house there are many dwelling places. If it were not so, would I have told you that I go to prepare a place for you? And if I go to prepare a place for you, I will come again and will take you to myself, so that where I am, there you may be also. And you know the way to the place where I am going." Thomas said to him, "Lord, we do not know where you are going. How can we know the way?" Jesus said to him, "I am the way, and the truth, and the life. No one comes to the Father except through me."

—JOHN 14:2–6

The story is told of a young man in upstate New York whose parents died when he was a teenager, leaving him with a vast fortune. As the young man came of age, he was highly sought after by many young women of social eminence.

So he devised a plan to find a bride who would love him for who he was—not what he had. He left home and took a train to Alabama, carrying only some working clothes in a cardboard suitcase.

He finally found a job in a factory, but he had never worked with his hands before. He was clumsy and awkward, and a young woman at the next table took pity on him. She showed him what to do and how to do it, helping him adjust to an uncomfortable situation.

He found her interesting and attractive. After a while, he explained that he had no folks, and he asked if he could visit her family. She asked her parents, who were both invalids, and they graciously invited the young man into their home.

She was working to support both her parents. She was industrious and had a pure heart. The young man fell in love with her and began to court her. After several months, he asked her father for permission to marry her. The father gave his consent, and the young woman said yes. She loved him deeply and looked forward to becoming his wife.

The couple wanted to do something special for their honeymoon, so they saved up enough money to buy train tickets to New York City. And finally, they boarded the train for the long trip north.

She had never left home before, and she was somewhat overwhelmed by Grand Central Station. And then, when they walked outside, a man in a uniform came up and picked up their suitcases.

"Stop him," she said to her husband. "That man is taking our luggage." But her husband assured her that it was all right. "It's just something special I want to do for you," he told her. And so, somewhat suspiciously, she followed the man with their bags to a limousine.

"Oh, we can't afford this," she protested.

"It's OK," he said. "It's just something special I want to do for you."

So they rode far out into the country and finally turned into a fenced estate, following a long, winding, tree-lined drive to the front of a palatial mansion. Now she knew they were well beyond their meager means, but he insisted everything would be OK. "Get out of the car," he said. "I have something I want to show you."

And then, on the porch, he pulled a key from his pocket, unlocked the door, and carried his bride across the threshold of her new home.

"This is yours," he said. "I have everything you need, and everything your parents need. You thought I was just a poor orphan, but I'm the heir to all this, and I want to share it all with you."

Someday the same thing will happen to the Church, which the Bible calls the Bride of Christ. Jesus will sweep us off our feet and carry us across the threshold of his heavenly estate. "You thought I was just a poor Nazarene carpenter," he will say. "But I'm the heir to all this, and I want to share it with you."

"It's just something very special I want to do for you."

God's Promise of Eternal Love

God's love is a sure thing that is always reaching out to us. This promise is cause for celebration.

Blest be the tie that binds
Our hearts in Christian love;
The fellowship of kindred minds
Is like to that above.
Before our Father's throne
We pour our ardent pray'rs;
Our fears, our hopes, our aims
    are one—
Our comforts and our cares.
When we asunder part
It gives us inward pain,
But we shall still be joined in
    heart,
And hope to meet again.

—JOHN FAWCETT

There's No Place Like God's Home

**As the Father has loved me, so I have loved
you; abide in my love. If you keep my
commandments, you will abide in my love,
just as I have kept my Father's
commandments and abide in his love.**
—JOHN 15:9–10

*M*ichelle has a problem: She has no
home. She's not homeless exactly. You
might say she has too many homes. When she
went to college, her parents lived in New Jersey.
That's where she grew up. But her parents just
moved to Michigan, and that has thrown her
emotions into turmoil.

"I don't have a *place* anymore, a place that's
really mine," she complains. Oh, the college
dorm is all right, but it's not really a home, just
a parking lot with beds and computers.
Michelle has friends in New Jersey, and she
could stay at a number of houses there, but
that state is not her home anymore, either. She
visits her parents on school vacations, but their
new house is strange to her, and she has to
bunk with her little sister. Michelle still helps
with the dishes, but she has to ask which cup-
boards they belong in. It's not her home.

Certainly there are worse problems to have. The poor who sleep in city parks won't have much sympathy for a young woman with three different places to live. And yet it's important to have a home, a place that's yours, somewhere you can abide.

That's the word Jesus used with his disciples in his farewell discourse at the Last Supper. Abide in my love. Sit down, kick your feet up, stay a while. Make yourself at home. The offer also extends to modern-day disciples. We can have a place in the heart of God. We can make our home there.

A home helps make you who you are. Your family instills certain values and habits, and

your neighborhood teaches you certain ways, too. We find distinct qualities in people from, say, New York or L.A., from the farm or the suburbs, from the Midwest or the deep South. We also see that children resemble their parents, not only in looks but in mannerisms, interests, and careers. Our homes mold us.

So when we find our spiritual home in the love of God, what does that mean? It means our lives are shaped by that love. We take comfort in God's love, and we share it with others. And, as Jesus says in these verses, we need to "keep his commandments." Not to earn God's love—that would be bribery—but as a loving response to the undeserved love we receive from God.

There are always house rules, in a college dorm or a suburban split-level, whether it's "No lacrosse in the halls" or "You take out the trash; I feed the dog." But the people who feel most at home don't mind the rules. Those rules are simply the way that a home functions best. It's the same way with God's love. For those who abide there, keeping the commandments comes naturally. Surrounded by love, we act with love.

A Simple Act of Kindness

Just one seemingly simple act of kindness can have far-reaching consequences. If we stop to help someone out, we might make their day—or even make a new friend.

*I*t was late Saturday afternoon when the pleasant-looking young lady with shoulder-length chestnut hair caught my attention—or rather the ankle-to-knee purple wrap over her leg cast caught it.

She was walking slowly on her crutches down the sloping sidewalk leading to the post office. I flashed a smile toward her as I reached for my car door, "That looks like a real pain," I called to her.

"You're right, it is," she chuckled. Then, reaching the bench in front of my car, she called back, "You wouldn't happen to have change for a $10 bill would you? I need to buy stamps from the machine."

"No, sorry. I only have a $20," I replied as I closed the door and put my key in the ignition.

"Oh well, I'll just sit here until someone comes along."

Stop. Elaine, you dummy. What's keeping you from running across the street to get change for her? The message came emblazoned across my conscience.

She was shocked to see me reopen the car door and walk toward her. "I'll be happy to run and get change for you from the grocery store."

"Oh, you don't have to do that. Someone will probably come with change pretty soon," she replied.

"I'd like to, really . . . it'll just take a minute. Wait a minute. Let me check the machine, first."

It took only three quick steps to reach the Post Office door and see the big "Out of Order" sign taped to the stamp dispenser. "Sorry, but there are no stamps here. The machine is out of order again."

In the next couple of minutes, we brainstormed other possibilities. But on our little northwest island, there appeared to be no other place to buy stamps.

Wait, Elaine. What's wrong with looking in your purse and giving her yours? There it was again— the still, small voice.

She was still talking to me, "That figures. I've had nothing but bad luck since I moved here. I nearly froze to death in that winter

storm. My landlord was in California, and I
had no water or electricity. Then I had this
accident, and now I can't even drive to get
around for another 45 days. People here are so
unfriendly. I'd be better off moving to another
state."

I breathed a quick prayer for just the right
words to respond to her. "Just a minute,"
I broke in. "I have stamps in my purse in the
car. Let me get them so you can mail the letters
that you need to today."

"I have 33 cents in
change. I can buy one
from you. Oh, and
here's my lucky silver
dollar. You can take
that, too," she said.

"No. I don't need
your money. Here—
take three or four
extra," I insisted as I
tore several from the
little book of stamps I'd retrieved from my car.

We chatted for a few more minutes, and I
learned that she lived less than a mile from me.
She had also become a volunteer cat and dog
walker at the Humane Society to help alleviate
her loneliness.

Give her your business card. There it was again—the still, small voice. I was getting more involved than I planned. Quickly, I went back to the car and got the card with my phone number.

"Listen, Denise (now I knew her name), I live near you. Give me a call if you need a ride to town. I come in at least twice a day, and I'd be happy to swing by and pick you up."

By this time she was reading my business card . . . Christian Writers Consultant, it said under my name. "Oh! You're a Christian. The other person who was nice to me this week was also a Christian, Rev. Baker, pastor at the Baptist church."

Sitting on the bench beside her, my schedule no longer seemed to matter as much as this lonely new neighbor. I was genuinely interested in her, her background, and her travels around the world. We talked another 20 minutes before I really had to go.

"I'll call you. Can we get together next week?" she asked when I stood to leave.

"Of course," I said. And as I drove away, I was smiling, not just at what had happened but with deep thankfulness for that still, small voice.

A Blessing of Love

May the blessing of God fill your days. Especially, may you develop the perfect balance of duties to family and responsibilities at work and worship. As you seek serenity in these things, may you find great cause for celebration, knowing that the one who loves you unconditionally remains at the center of all your activity.

Lovable Differences

Bless our differences, O Lord. And let us love across all barriers—the walls we build of color, culture, and language. Let us turn our eyes upward and remember: The God who made all of us lives and breathes and moves within us, untouched by our petty distinctions. Let us love him as he is, for he loves us just as we are.

Blessed Friendship

May you come to know that God is your friend. When you feel a frowning face is looking down at you from heaven, recall that nothing you could do could ever make God love you more or love you less. He simply loves— completely and perfectly. So feel the blessedness of his love!

To Love Brings Happiness

We reflect the goodness of God most when we love others. It is life's highest, and sometimes most difficult, goal.

Lord, we thank you for showering your love upon our lives and giving us the strength and desire to share it with those we love.

Too Great a Gift to Keep

Some gifts are simply too special to keep to ourselves. The great storyteller Bob Benson tells this story of an African man who shared his greatest gift with others.

I once heard a missionary tell a very moving story about an African man to whom he had given a copy of the Bible. The African  was so grateful for that gift, and so profuse in his thanks, that the missionary was puzzled a few months later when they met again. For the Bible was battered and torn and it looked as though many of the pages were missing.

"I thought you would have taken better care of the Bible I gave you," he remarked. "I assumed you wanted it and would treasure it."

And the African man replied, "It is the finest gift I ever received. It is such a wonderful book that I gave a page to my father and a page to my mother and then I gave a page to everyone in the village."

—BOB BENSON, *SEE YOU AT THE HOUSE*

Surprised by Grace

But, as it is written, "No eye has seen,
nor ear heard, nor the human
heart conceived, what God has prepared
for those who love him."
—1 CORINTHIANS 2:9

My son thinks it is great fun to hide behind a door or a chair and jump out and surprise us. We usually jump, let out a scream, and get mildly annoyed at our beloved child. Yet, I do not think that such a surprise is on quite the scale that Paul is talking about in his letter to the Corinthians.

Most scholars believe that Paul is quoting from chapter 64 of Isaiah, where the prophet is testifying that there is no God like the God of the Israelites. No one has ever seen or heard of a God who does such wonderful deeds for a group of people, who welcomes people who delight in doing what is right. Paul is quoting the prophet to show the Corinthian people that God is truly amazing. Furthermore, Paul can tell them even more about God's love known in Jesus Christ because the Holy Spirit has revealed God's wisdom to Paul.

God is truly surprising, doing what no eye
has seen nor ear has heard. Paul isn't talking
about a magic act, but about the way God
works through Jesus Christ. We have a Sunday
at church called Amazing Grace Sunday. It is a
day we invite a member of the congregation to
tell about God's amazing grace in his or her
life. The stories told are filled with trials and
pains, addictions and illnesses, but always there
is the surprising action of God working for
good. At the end of a long bout with drinking
or in the middle of brain surgery, one would
not expect the story to turn out all right. Yet,
God is able to do what no eye has seen nor
heart has conceived.

We always finish the worship service
singing "Amazing Grace." That song was written by John Newton, a former captain of a
slave-trader ship, who was surprised by the love
of God and gave up slave trading for the chance
to tell people about the surprising mercy of
God. At that service we celebrate the abundant
life that is available to each one of us in surprising ways.

Sometimes we don't trust that God is surprising us with blessings and opportunities.
I have a friend who loves the theater. She has
taught acting, directed plays, and is forever

dreaming of going on stage herself. Not long ago, she was offered a part in a professional production. Yet, instead of being elated, she was nervous and hesitant. She said, "I am afraid of success." She is very talented, and now God has not only blessed her with ability, but he has also blessed and surprised her with an opportunity to use that talent. She is having to work through past experiences of disappointment and rejection so she can trust herself to embrace the abundant life now.

It is important to celebrate the surprising blessings of God. Sometimes we take God's abundant grace for granted, or we are so sure that we know the way that God will act. We lose the ability to see the surprising ways God is at work around us. There are other times we tend to focus on the pains and problems of life. In the old days, there were testimonies in churches. I think they went out of fashion when the same folks repeated the same testimonies. They lost their freshness, but the time may be ripe to recover the tradition of brief expressions of God's abundant grace. May we never lose our openness to be surprised by God's love.

We plow the fields and scatter
The good seed on the land,
But it is fed and watered
By God's almighty hand;
He sends the snow in winter,
The warmth to swell the grain,
The breezes and the sunshine,
And soft, refreshing rain.
All good gifts around us
Are sent from heaven above:
Then thank the Lord,
O thank the Lord
For all His love.

—MATHIAS CLAUDIUS, "WE PLOW THE
FIELDS AND SCATTER THE GOOD SEED"

For a Helper

As you launch out in this helping venture, may you continually recall that charity begins, but does not end, at home. That is why you are going.

When you seem to lose all your energy, when you've given all you can, rest in God's strength. When you come to the end of your rope, and patience seems to fly away, settle back in God's waiting arms.

Make times of peace and quiet for yourself!

And when you feel as though you'd like to quit and go home, persevere in the light of God's long-standing love for you over the years.

In all this hard work, rely not on your own willpower, but discover the blessing of being in need. For this is the only way you will succeed, and it is the only way for others to have the opportunity to do something kind for you. Along with them—be blessed by our loving God!

God gave because he is love. It was the best he had to offer. The supreme gift. The total gift. In the person of his Son, he gave himself.

Youth and Consequences

**For you, O Lord, are my hope, my trust, O
Lord, from my youth.**
—PSALM 71:5

"Is that all there is?" singer Peggy Lee asked
in her tribute to disappointment, in which
all sorts of childhood hopes are dashed, and
there's nothing left to do but keep dancing.

For all too many, that's the story of their
lives. They grew up believing, trusting, and
hoping, but then adulthood struck them like a
cement truck. They had a painful romance, and
they've stopped believing in love. They studied
science or philosophy, and they've stopped
trusting God. They got stuck in a dead-end job,
and they've stopped hoping for the future.

"Is that all there is?"

The psalmist sings praises to God as his
"hope," indicating that he has trusted the Lord
since he was young. It's not surprising that he
trusted God as a child, since children tend to
be trusting. It's more amazing that he's still
trusting God as an adult. Didn't he ever have

his faith shaken? Didn't he ever face disillusionment that made him lose his religion?

The previous verse puts the psalmist in "the grasp of the unjust and cruel." Things are not going well for him, but he maintains his hope in God. Maybe you've heard of "tough love." This is tough hope.

People have the idea that faith is kid stuff. Hope is a sweet outlook for a child, but adults get cynical. "When you know better, boys and girls, you'll stop expecting so much out of life."

Maybe that's why Jesus said we had to become like little children to enter God's kingdom. We need to rub the calluses off our hearts and dare to dream again. In spite of all the pain we've been through, we need to trust in God, who loves us, who will make everything all right, eventually, according to his time and his plan.

And if we take our cue from the psalmist, it's not about philosophy or science, it's not even about our dreams or goals; it's about our personal relationship with God. Note how the psalmist doesn't say that God gives him hope, though surely he does. No, the Lord *is* his hope. The believer does not trust in some pretty picture of life here on earth or hereafter, but in a living, loving Lord.

*F*or I am convinced that
nothing can ever separate us
from his love. Death can't, and
life can't. The angels won't, and
all the powers of hell itself
cannot keep God's love away.
Our fears for today, our worries
about tomorrow, or where we
are—high above the sky, or in the
deepest ocean—nothing will ever
be able to separate us from the
love of God demonstrated by our
Lord Jesus Christ when
he died for us.

—ROMANS 8:38-39 (TLB)